Copyright 2020 by On Williams Street
Written and Published by
Kimberlee Tanner and Melissa Winona
www.onwilliamsstreet.com

Do not Copy or Distribute without Written Permission

Welcome!

This book came about when we started making quilt blocks for magnets. It was so much fun using scraps to make these tiny blocks, we wanted to make more! After brainstorming and playing, we decided that it was the perfect opportunity to do our own modern take on an I Spy quilt. Lots of discussing and input from our family and friends and we soon had a list of over 100 ideas for blocks.

After we had compiled our list, it came time to design. We wanted to include ideas from lots of different categories to provide a fun and varied quilt that appeals to all! Whether you are using the blocks all together in one quilt, or mixing and matching for all sorts of project opportunities, we are sure you'll find something for the loved ones on your quilting list!

Who We Are
Kimie and Missy

We are two sisters that share a passion for quilting. Seven years ago, we found ourselves at a crossroads. We had been talking about designing quilt patterns together, but we had never made it actually happen. In early 2013 that all changed! We released our first few patterns and haven't looked back since. If we aren't quilting, you can usually find us creating in other ways like building furniture or cooking yummy treats. We are so grateful for your support and hope you love this book as much as we do!

Table of Contents

From tools, to the blocks, to putting it all together, this book has it all. Check out the Getting Started section for the tools and instructions needed for Foundation Paper Piecing, then jump right in wherever you want to start!

4 Getting Started

Some tools are required, others just make things easier. Read this section first if you are new to foundation paper piecing.

10 Around the House

All the fun things you find yourself using each and every day.

18 Playtime

It's time to play! Grab a ball or crayon and get ready to have a blast!

26 Getting Ready

Hair, check. Teeth brushed, check. Lipstick, check! ! We are ready to go.

32 Dress Up

Jump in the pool or build a snowman. We have clothes for every occasion.

40 Animals

Farm animals, sea animals, and more!

Sandcastle
x — x — x — x

So many blocks, so little time. If you don't know where to start, either start at the beginning, or make all the level ones first.

Of course, you can also just pick your favorite! Either way, it's going to be adorable when you finish.

91

52 Let's Celebrate

We love to celebrate. What is your favorite holiday?

66 In the Garden

It's time to dig in the dirt and get dirty. Plant flowers, find bugs, or just enjoy being outdoors.

79 On the Move

By train, plane, or boat, we don't care, we just want to go!

86 On Vacation

Spend some quiet time away and unwind from all your worries.

95 Let's Eat

Dinner is ready! Grab a plate and fill it up with all sorts of yummy things to eat.

110 Putting it All Together

Now that the blocks are done, it's time to make a quilt. Don't worry, this is the easy part.

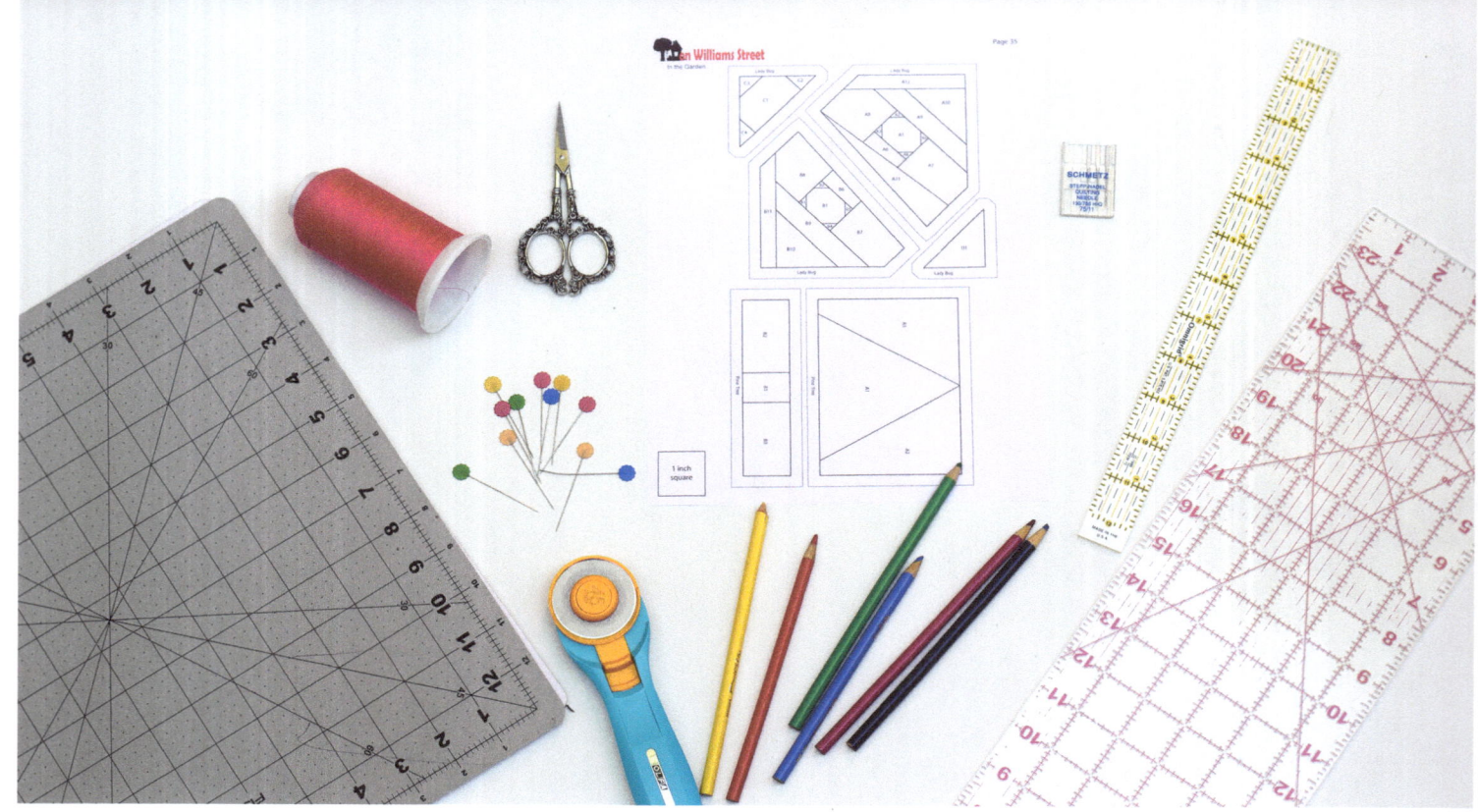

Getting Started

Each block finishes at 4" square. It should be 4 1/2" square with the outside seam allowance. The final quilt measures approximately 51" square.

Tools

1 - Basic Sewing Machine
For this quilt you don't need a machine with fancy stitches, just a basic straight stitch and the ability to decrease the length of that stitch.

2 - Thread
For foundation paper piecing we recommend using a thinner thread. This will help reduce seam bulk. We use either Superior Threads So Fine! or Superior Threads Micro Quilter.

3 - Needle
Nothing fancy here, we use a basic all-purpose sewing needle.

4 - Cutting Mat
When it comes to cutting mats, we say the bigger the better, but you can easily complete this quilt with a mat that is about 17 x 23".

5 - Rotary Cutter
There are lots to choose from, find the one that you prefer and make sure it has a good sharp blade.

6 - Scissors
Lots of options here as well. You just need a good pair of sharp scissors. We love our Ginghers.

7 - Pins
Just good old fashioned straight pins work great. But all the fun new pins with flower, unicorn, heart, star, etc heads can also be a necessity if you want them to. We may need to start a pin collection with all the fun things they keep coming out with.

8 - 1 x 12" Ruler
This is a must when it comes to tools in our toolbox. We use it for so many things but it is very handy for foundation paper piecing. We'll show you why in our basic instructions.

9 - 6 x 24" Ruler
This really is a must have for all quilters. It makes cutting those sashing and border strips so much easier. And if you want to make it even easier, you add the Guildelines 4 Quitling ruler guide to it. We use our guide on a daily basis.

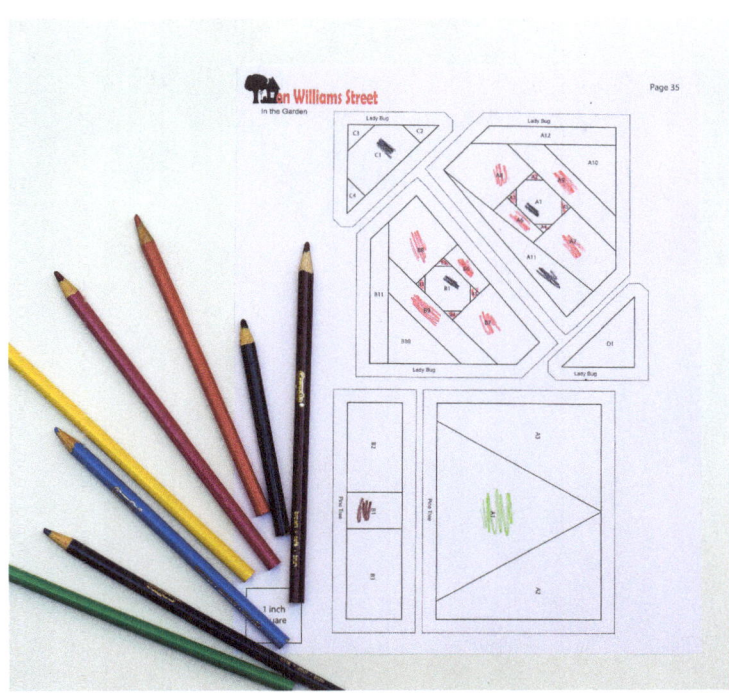

10 - Light Box – optional
This isn't a necessity, but if you are new to foundation paper piecing and are worried about making sure your fabric covers your template correctly, it can help ease that stress. And it doesn't need to be fancy, even a sunny window works well.

11 - Pen or Pencil (preferably colored)
This will help you as you layout the templates and determine colors for each section. We like to use colored pencils and color in each section with the color of fabric we need for it.

12 - Copies of the templates
Well, it would be hard to make the quilt without the templates, but we want to make sure you have a good comprehensive list of tools and supplies.

Printing the Templates

To print the templates,
head to: **www.onwilliamsstreet.com/ispytemplates**, Password: **letscreate!**

When printing, make sure that you are printing at 100%. Some printers will say "no scaling", others will show the percentage of size. If there is an option to "fit to page", we DO NOT want this. Even just a little size difference in the templates will make a big difference over all 100 blocks and your sizing will be off. Use the 1" square box to check that your templates are the correct size before starting. The one inch mark on your ruler should line up perfectly on the box lines.

Fabric Requirements

1 1/4 yards White Sashing and Border
3 1/2 yards of White background
1/2 Binding
3 1/4 Backing

Lots of colored scraps

If you are new to quilting or don't have a stash or scrap collection yet, we recommend using 3-4 sets of charm packs (40-50 charms each) in solids or tone on tone selections to give you the most variety of choices. You'll need an assortment of reds, greens, purples, blues, pinks, yellows, oranges, browns, tans, turquoises, and grays in light, medium and dark shades as well as black.

Note: There should be enough leftover backing to bind your quilt if you want to use the same fabric.

Using the Block Guides

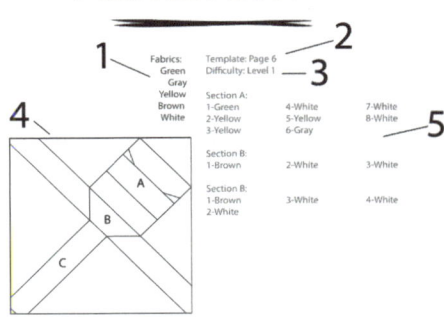

1 - Fabrics: The colors needed to complete the block.

2 - Page number: This is the template page you'll find the block on for printing.

3 - Difficulty level: If you are new to foundation paper piecing, start with level one blocks and work up from there.

4 - Piecing diagram: Use this for blocks with multiple pieces when arranging and sewing them together.

5 - Color Key: What color goes where.

Making Each Block

- You have all your supplies gathered and now its time to start. The first step that we recommend completing is printing your templates and coloring in each section. This eliminates unpicking because you grabbed the wrong color of fabric for a section of the block. This is a lesson that we have learned more than once.

- Cut out each of the templates, making sure not to cut into that 1/4" seam line.

- Gather the fabrics that you need for each block.

- If you are new to Foundation Paper Piecing, don't worry, by the time you complete all the blocks, you'll be an expert. You will want to start with the blocks labeled as level 1. Once you complete these, you will be ready to move on to the level 2 blocks then to the advanced level 3 blocks.

- Your template will be printed in reverse. The right side of the fabric will be facing up from the underside of the template with all seams enclosed between the fabric and template.

- Decrease your stitch length. We use about a 1.5 setting on our machine. This will make it easier to remove the paper after completing the block.

- When joining blocks with multiple sections, first join section A to B, then add C, then D, E, etc as needed.

- Press your sections with an iron before you trim to the final size, this will help things lay flat and give you a true to size finished section. You don't have to press with an iron for every seam in each section unless you prefer. A good finger press works here.

- You can either remove the paper from each section before or after sewing them together. Leaving the paper on can help with lining things up, but in some cases you'll end up with little pieces in the seams that are hard to remove (don't worry too much about these, they will disintegrate in the wash). We recommend you experiment with both ways to see what you prefer.

How to Foundation Paper Piece

If you are new to foundation paper piecing, or just need a refresher, follow the simple steps below to complete each block. When you are ready to start on the quilt, begin with blocks labeled level one and then work up to the harder blocks.

Step 1—Locate first template. (Fig A)

Step 2—Locate pieces 1 and 2 on your template. Completely cover piece 1 with fabric from the back of the template, ensuring the right side of the fabric is facing up.

Make sure to leave at least 1/4" all around the piece. (Fig B)

Step 3— Measure fabric for piece 2, checking that it completely covers the piece and allows for a 1/4" allowance around the piece.

Line up the fabric for piece 2, on top of piece 1, right sides together. (Fig B) Pin as needed to keep both pieces in place.

Turn template over and sew along the line separating piece 1 and piece 2. Turn back to fabric side and finger press open. (Fig C)

Fold back template on the line separating piece 1 and 2 from piece 3 and trim fabric to 1/4" seam from the line. This is where the 1" ruler comes in handy.

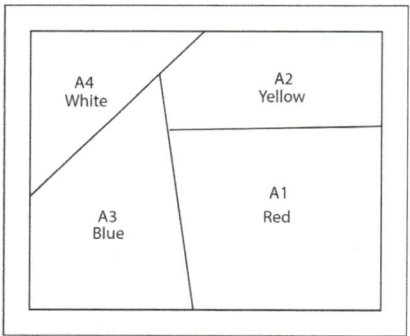

Fig A

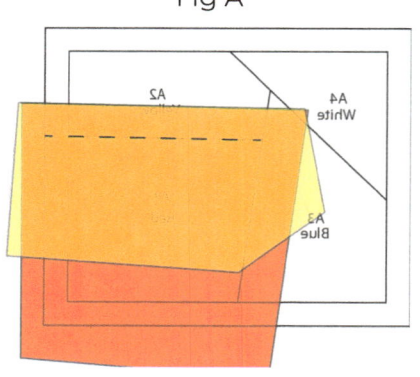

Fig B

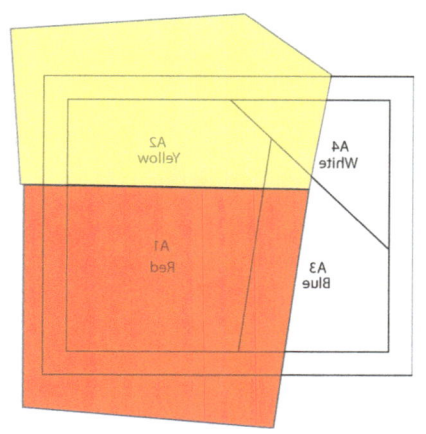

Fig C

Step 4— Measure fabric for piece 3, checking that it completely covers the piece and allows for a 1/4" allowance around the piece.

Line up the fabric for piece 3 with piece 1 and 2, right sides together. Pin as needed. (Fig D)

Turn template over and sew along the line separating piece 1, 2, and 3. Turn back to fabric side and finger press open. (Fig E)

Fold back template on the line separating piece 3 from piece 4 and trim fabric to 1/4" seam from the line.

Step 5—Repeat as needed for the remainder of the section. (Fig F and G)

Press the entire section with an iron. Turn to the paper side and trim entire section to final dimensions, leaving the final 1/4" seam allowance. (Fig H and I)

Step 6—Following the instructions on the pattern, sew individual sections together.

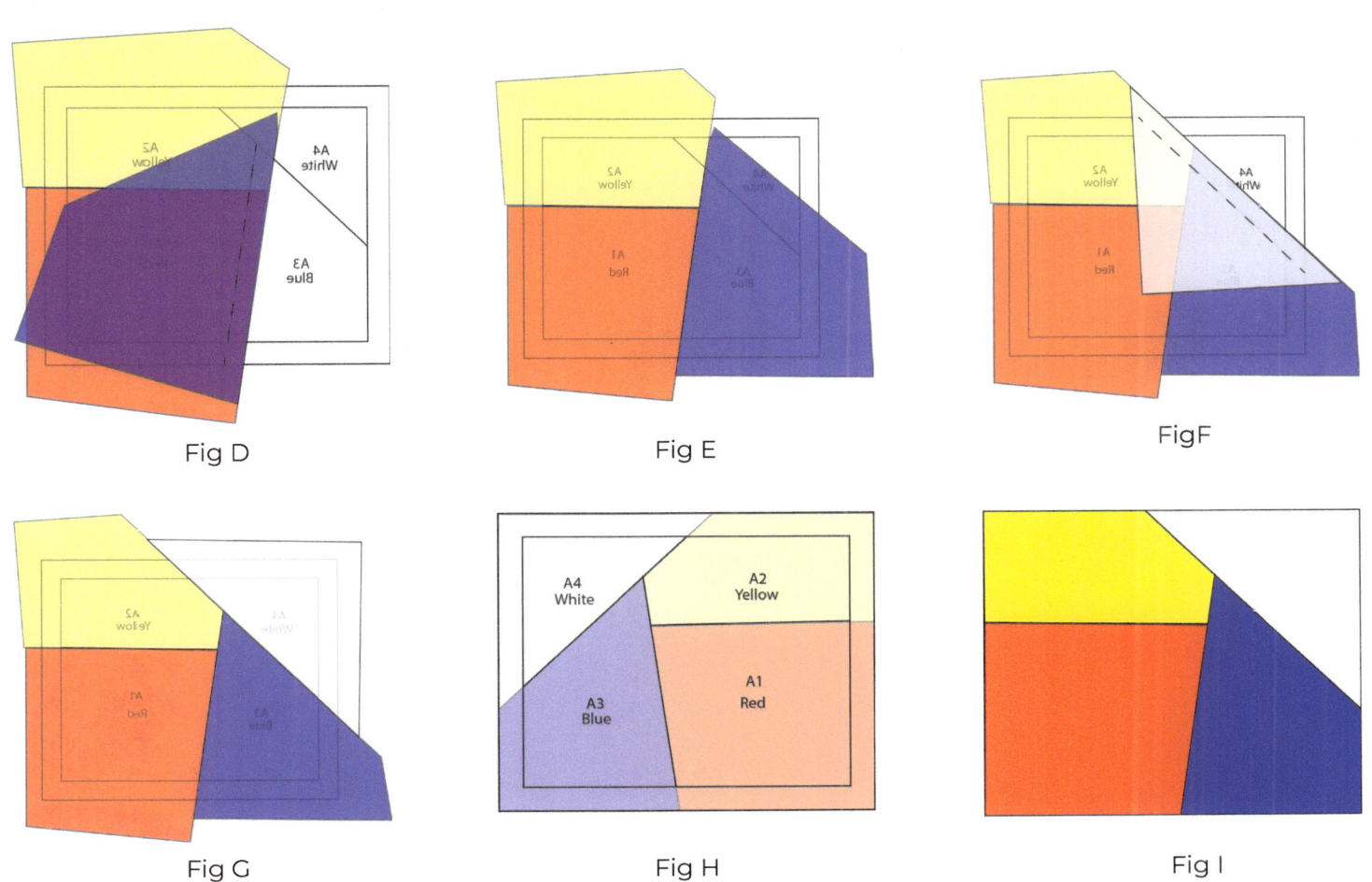

Fig D   Fig E   Fig F

Fig G   Fig H   Fig I

Phone

Fabrics:
Black
White

Template: Page 1
Difficulty: Level 2

Section A:
1-White	5-Black	9-White
2-Black	6-Black	10-White
3-Black	7-Black	11-White
4-Black	8-Black	12-White

Section B:
1-White	4-Black	7-Black
2-Black	5-White	8-White
3-Black	6-White	9-White

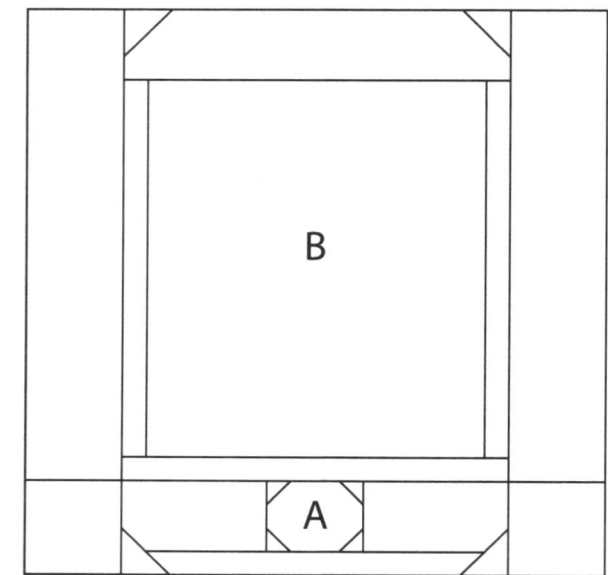

Teacup

Fabrics:
Turquoise
White

Template: Page 1
Difficulty: Level 2

Section A:
1-Turquoise   3-White   4-White
2-White

Section B:
1-Turquoise   2-White   3-White

Section C:
1-White   6-Turquoise   11-White
2-Turquoise   7-Turquoise   12-White
3-Turquoise   8-Turquoise   13-White
4-Turquoise   9-Turquoise   14-White
5-Turquoise   10-White   15-White

Lamp

Fabrics:
Gold
Light Gray
Purple
White

Template: Page 2
Difficulty: Level 2

Section A:
1-Lt Gray	3-White	5-Gold
2-White	4-White	6-White

Section B:
1-Gold	3-White	5-White
2-White	4-White	

Section C:
1-Purple	2-White	3-White

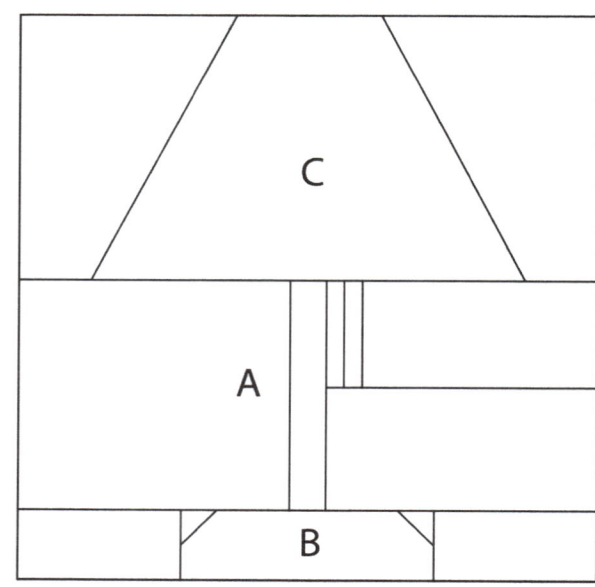

Broom

Fabrics:
Red
Black
White

Template: Page 2
Difficulty: Level 2

Section A:
1-Red   2-White   3-White

Section B:
1-Red   2-White   3-White

Section C:
1-Black   2-White   3-White

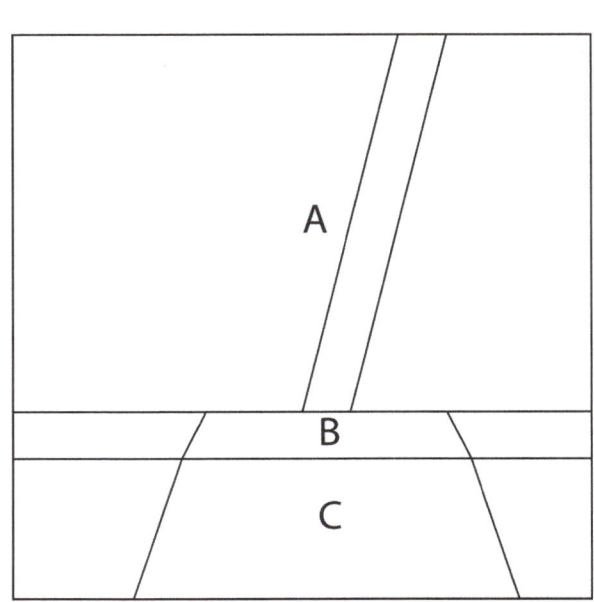

House

~~~~~~~~~~~

Fabrics:
Blue
Red
Gray
White

Template: Page 3
Difficulty: Level 1

Section A:
1-Gray   3-Blue   5-White
2-Blue   4-Blue   6-White

Section B:
1-Red   2-White   3-White

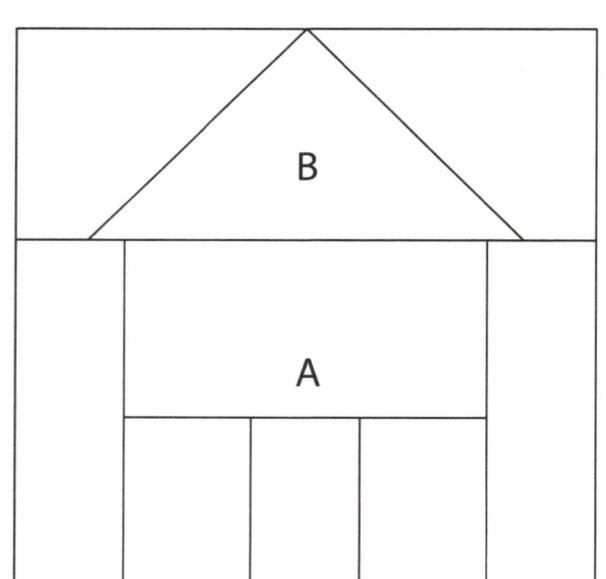

Fork

Fabrics:
Gray
White

Template: Page 3
Difficulty: Level 2

Section A:
1-Gray
2-White
3-White
4-Gray
5-Gray
6-Gray
7-White
8-White
9-White
10-White

Section B:
1-Gray
2-White
3-White
4-Gray
5-Gray
6-White

Section C:
1-Gray
2-White
3-White
4-White

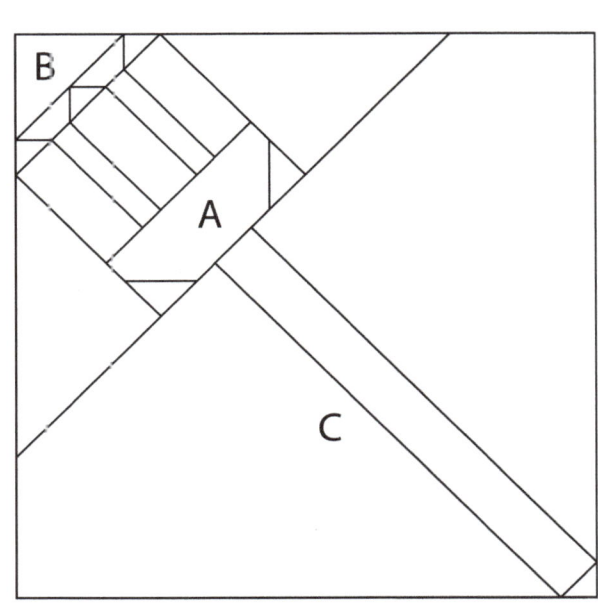

Floppy Disk

Fabrics:
Turquoise
Gray
White

Template: Page 4
Difficulty: Level 1

Section A:
1-Gray	4-Gray	7-White
2-Turquoise	5-Gray	8-Turquoise
3-Gray	6-Turquoise	9-Turquoise

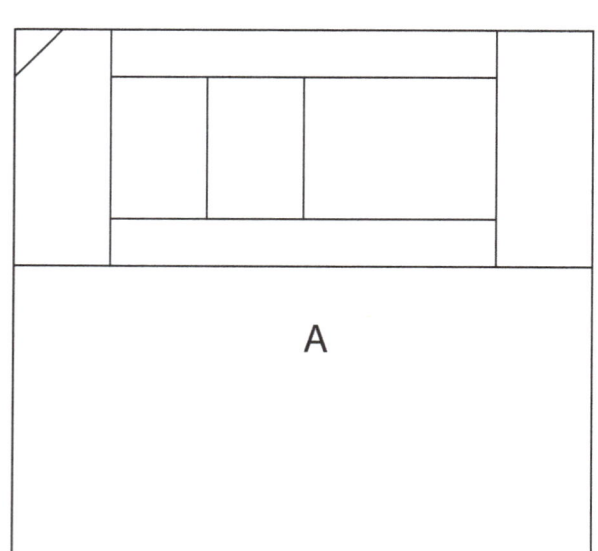

Teapot

Fabrics:
Yellow
Light Yellow
White

Template: Page 4
Difficulty: Level 3

Section A:
1-Lt Yellow
2-White
3-White
4-White
5-White

Section B:
1-Yellow
2-White
3-White
4-White
5-White
6-White
7-White

Section C:
1-Yellow
2-White
3-White
4-White
5-White
6-White
7-White
8-White

Section D:
1-Yellow
2-White
3-White
4-White
5-White

Section E:
1-Lt Yellow
2-White
3-Lt Yellow
4-White
5-White

Section F:
1-White
2-Lt Yellow
3-Lt Yellow
4-Lt Yellow
5-Lt Yellow
6-White
7-White
8-White
9-White
10-White
11-White

Gumball Machine

Fabrics:
Red
Light Gray
Dark Gray
White

Template: Page 5
Difficulty: Level 2

Section A:
1-Dk Gray	4-Red	7-White
2-Red	5-Red	8-White
3-Red	6-Red	

Section B:
1-Lt Gray	4-White	7-White
2-White	5-White	
3-White	6-White	

Section C:
1-Red   2-White   3-White

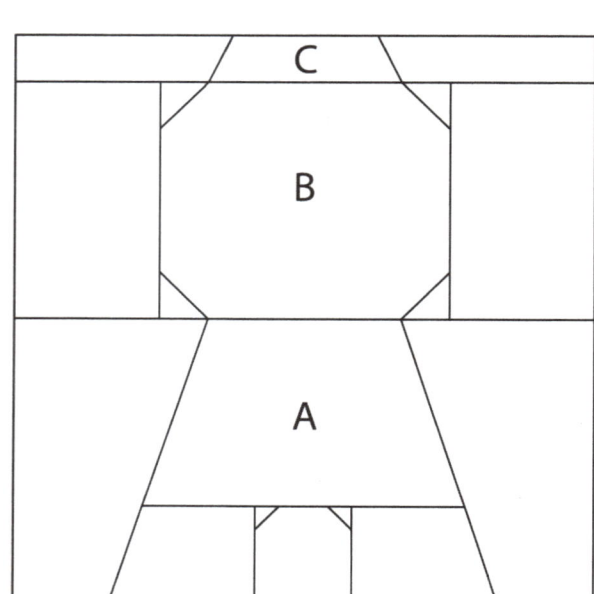

Baseball Bat

O – O – O – O – O

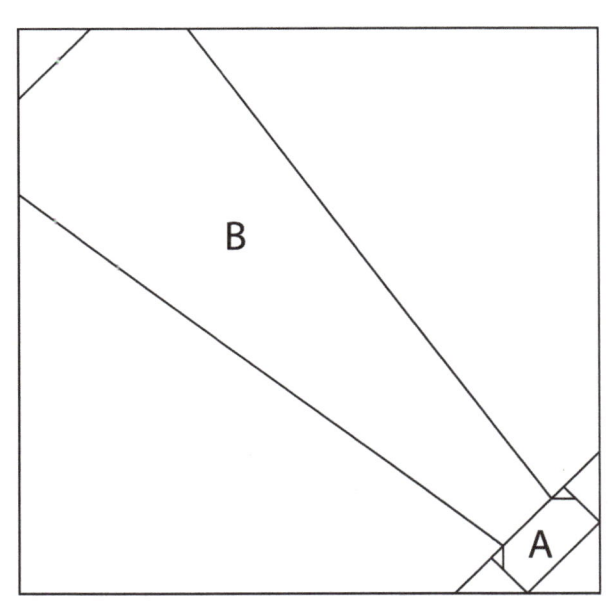

Fabrics:
Brown
White

Template: Page 5
Difficulty: Level 1

Section A:
| 1-Brown | 3-White | 5-White |
| 2-White | 4-White | 6-White |

Section B:
| 1-Brown | 3-White | 4-White |
| 2-White | | |

Pencil

Fabrics:
Yellow
Tan
Black
Gray
Pink
White

Template: Page 6
Difficulty: Level 2

Section A:
1-Yellow	6-Tan	11-White
2-Tan	7-Black	12-White
3-Yellow	8-Yellow	13-White
4-Tan	9-Gray	
5-Yellow	10-Pink	

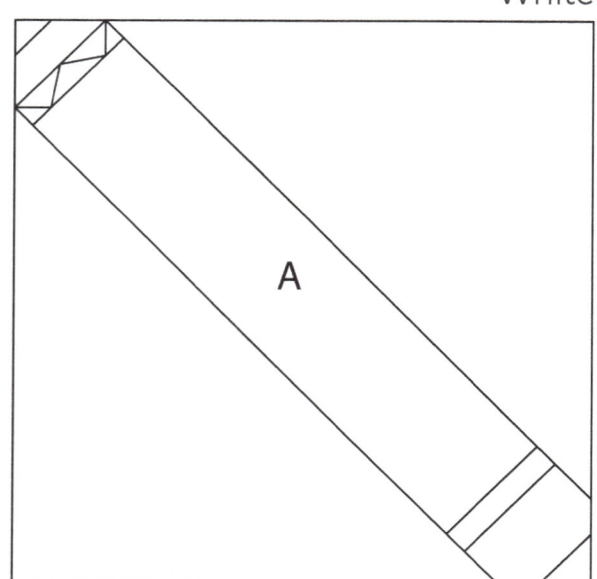

20

Paintbrush

Fabrics:
Green
Gray
Yellow
Brown
White

Template: Page 6
Difficulty: Level 1

Section A:
1-Green	4-White	7-White
2-Yellow	5-Yellow	8-White
3-Yellow	6-Gray	

Section B:
1-Brown	2-White	3-White

Section C:
1-Brown	3-White	4-White
2-White		

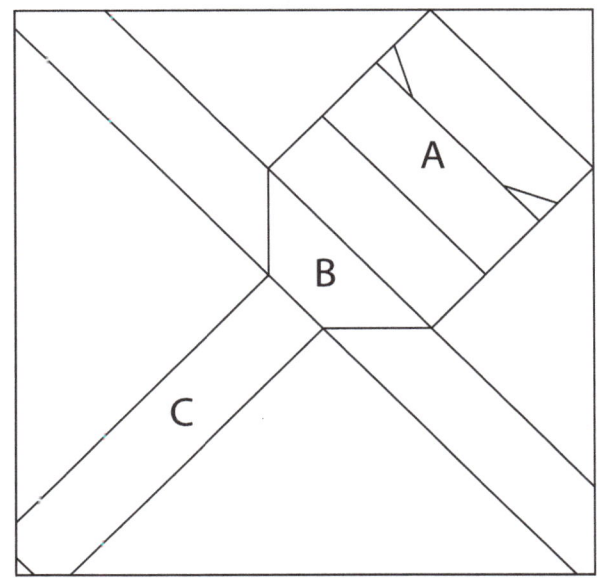

Basketball

~~~~~~~~~~

Fabrics:
Black
Orange
White

Template: Page 7
Difficulty: Level 2

Section A:
1-Black
2-Orange
3-Orange
4-Black

Section B:
1-Black
2-Orange
3-Orange

Section C:
1-Black
2-Orange
3-Orange
4-Black
5-Black
6-Orange
7-White
8-Black
9-Orange
10-White

Section D
1-Black
2-Orange
3-Orange
4-Black
5-Black
6-Orange
7-White
8-Black
9-Orange
10-White

Crayon

Fabrics:
Purple
Light Purple
Black
White

Template: Page 7
Difficulty: Level 2

Section A:
1-Black
2-Lt Purple
3-Lt Purple
4-Lt Purple
5-Lt Purple
6-Lt Purple
7-Lt Purple
8-Lt Purple
9-Black
10-Lt Purple
11-Purple
12-White
13-Lt Purple
14-Black
15-Lt Purple
16-Purple
17-White
18-White

Section B:
1-Purple
2-White
3 -White

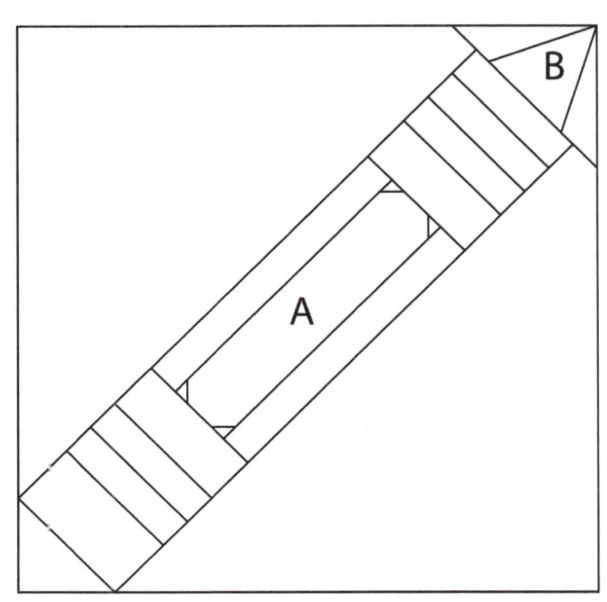

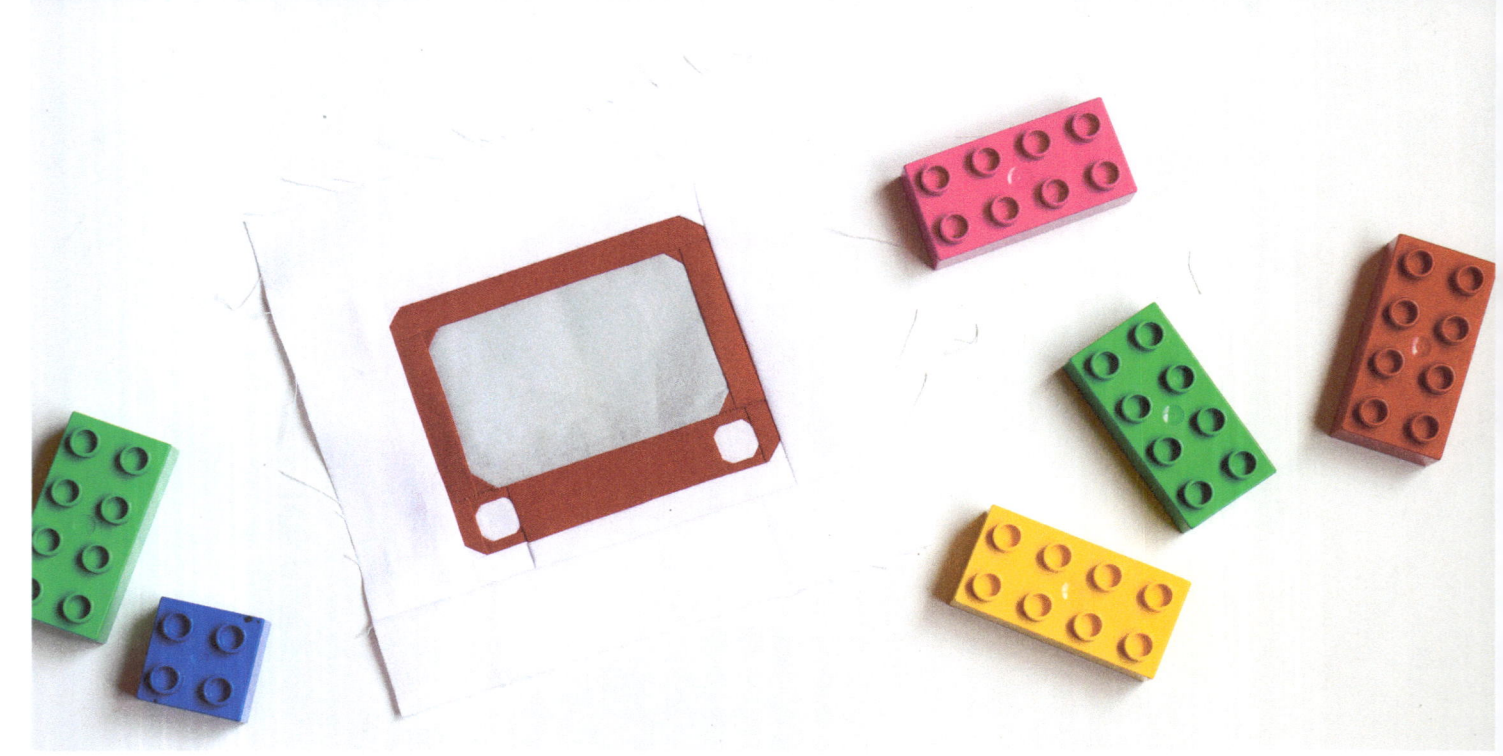

Drawing Toy

Fabrics:
Red
Gray
White

Template: Page 8
Difficulty: Level 3

Section A:
1-White	5-Red	9-White
2-Red	6-Red	10-White
3-Red	7-Red	
4-Red	8-Red	

Section B:
1-White	5-Red	9-White
2-Red	6-Red	10-Red
3-Red	7-Red	11-White
4-Red	8-Red	

Section C:
1-Gray	5-Red	9-White
2-Red	6-Red	10-White
3-Red	7-Red	11-White
4-Red	8-Red	

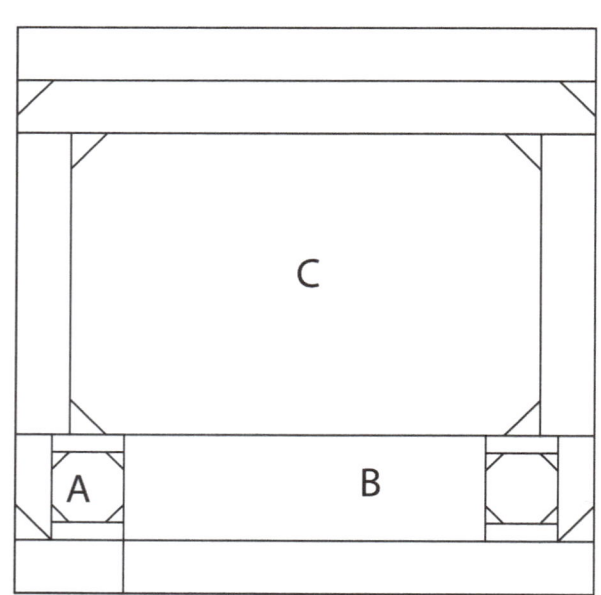

Football

o x o x o x o x

Fabrics:
Brown
White

Template: Page 8
Difficulty: Level 2

Section A:
1-Brown
2-White
3-White
4-Brown
5-White
6-Brown
7-White
8-Brown
9-White
10-Brown
11-White
12-Brown
13-White
14-White
15-Brown
16-White
17-White

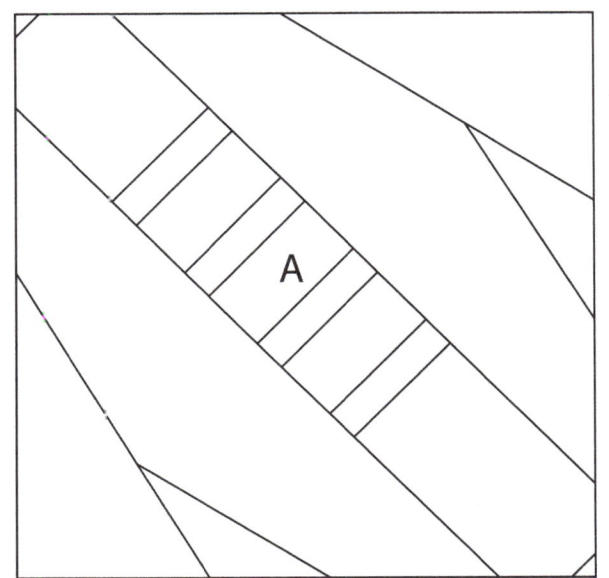

Hair Dryer

Fabrics:
Pink
Dark Gray
Gray
White

Template: Page 9
Difficulty: Level 3

Section A:
1-Pink	6-Dk Gray	11-White
2-Dk Gray	7-Dk Gray	12-White
3-Dk Gray	8-Dk Gray	13-White
4-Dk Gray	9-Dk Gray	14-White
5-Dk Gray	10-White	15-White

Section B:
1-Gray	4-Dk Gray	7-White
2-Dk Gray	5-Dk Gray	8-White
3-Dk Gray	6-White	9-White

Section C:
1-Dk Gray		
2-White	3-White	4-White

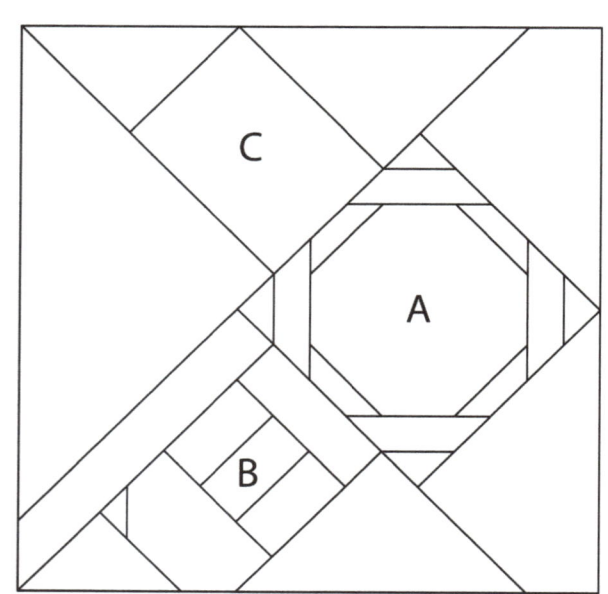

Comb

Fabrics:
Black
White

Template: Page 9
Difficulty: Level 2

Section A:

1-White	8-White	15-Black
2-Black	9-Black	16-White
3-Black	10-White	17-Black
4-White	11-Black	18-White
5-Black	12-White	19-White
6-White	13-Black	
7-Black	14-White	

Section B:

1-Black	3-White	5-White
2-White	4-White	

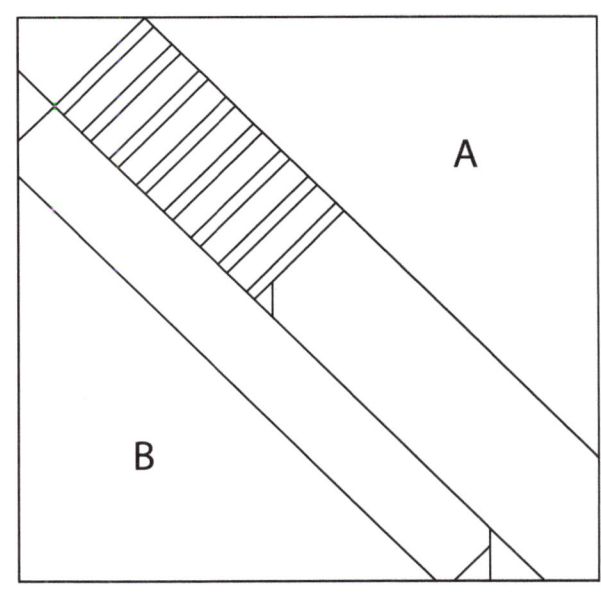

Mirror

Fabrics:
Yellow
Light Gray
White

Template: Page 10
Difficulty: Level 2

Section A:
1-Lt Gray	6-Yellow	11-White
2-Yellow	7-White	12-White
3-Yellow	8-Yellow	13-White
4-Yellow	9-Yellow	14-White
5-Yellow	10-White	15-White

Section B:
1-Lt Gray	3-Yellow	5-White
2-Yellow	4-Yellow	6-White

Section C:
1-Yellow	3-White	4-White
2-White		

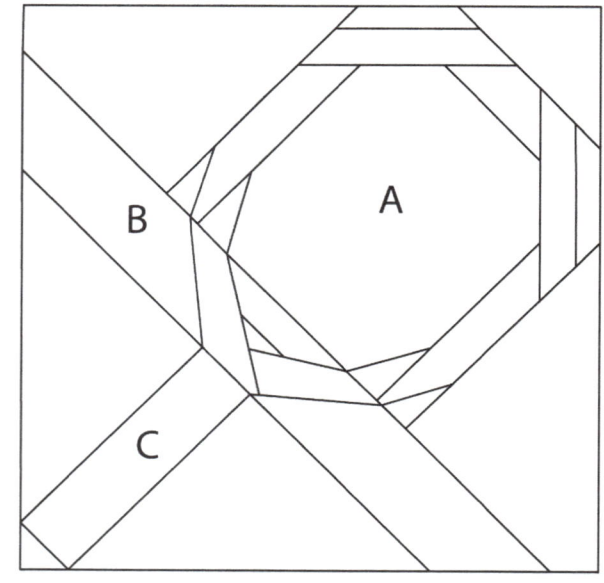

Lipstick

Fabrics:
Red
Black
White

Template: Page 10
Difficulty: Level 2

Section A:
1-Red
2-White
3-White
4-White
5-White

Section B:
1-Black
2-White
3-White

Section C:
1-Black
2-White
3-White
4-White

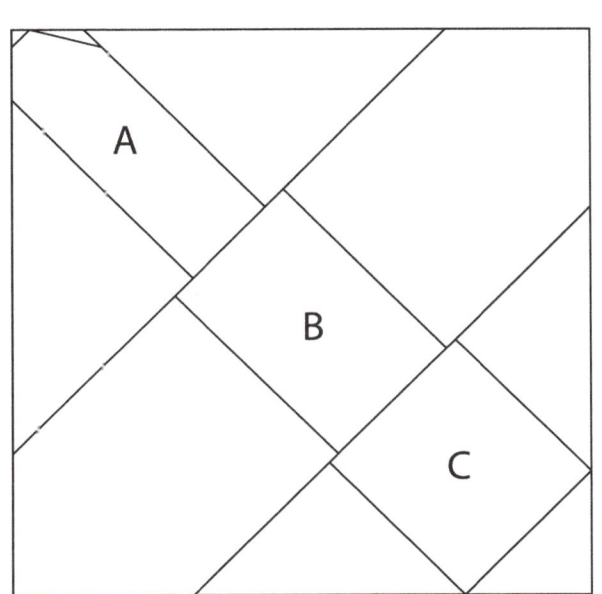

Nail Polish

~~~

Fabrics:
Pink
Black
White

Template: Page 11
Difficulty: Level 2

Section A:
1-Pink	4-White	7-White
2-White	5-White	
3-White	6-White	

Section B:
1-Black	3-White	5-White
2-White	4-White	

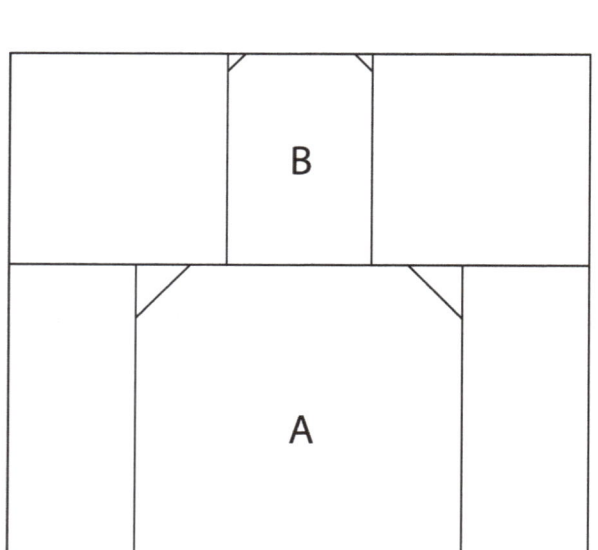

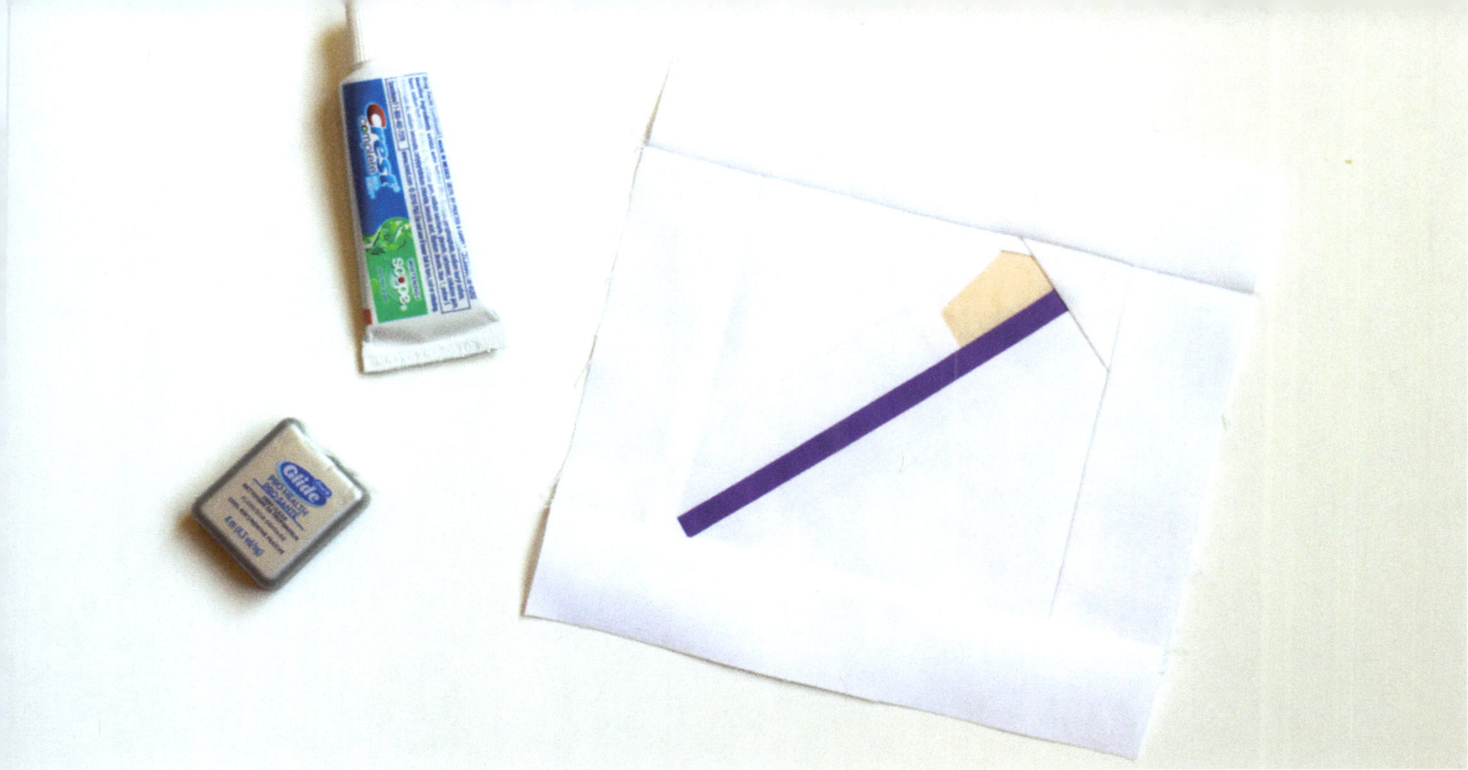

Toothbrush

Fabrics:
Purple
Light Gray
White

Template: Page 11
Difficulty: Level 1

Section A:
1-Lt Gray	4-White	7-White
2-White	5-White	8-White
3-White	6-Purple	9-White

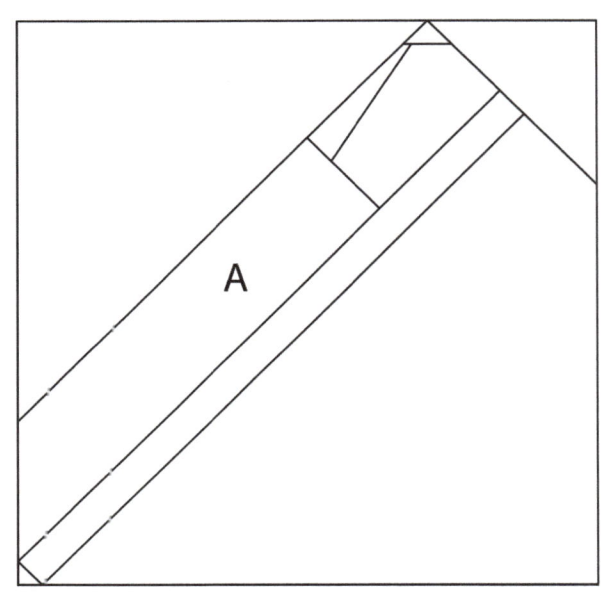

31

Snow Hat

Fabrics:
Pink
Light Pink
White

Template: Page 12
Difficulty: Level 2

Section A:
1-Lt Pink 4-Lt Pink 7-White
2-Pink   5-Pink   8-White
3-Pink   6-White   9-White

Section B:
1-Lt Pink 4-White 7-White
2-White   5-White
3-White   6-White

Section C:
1-Pink   3-White 5-White
2-White   4-White

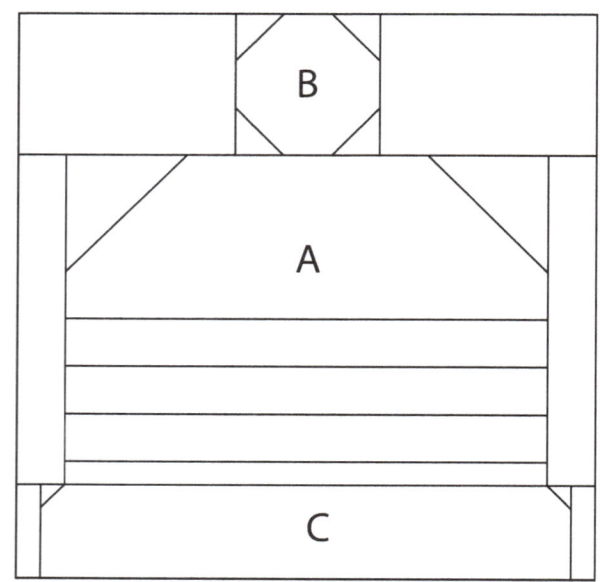

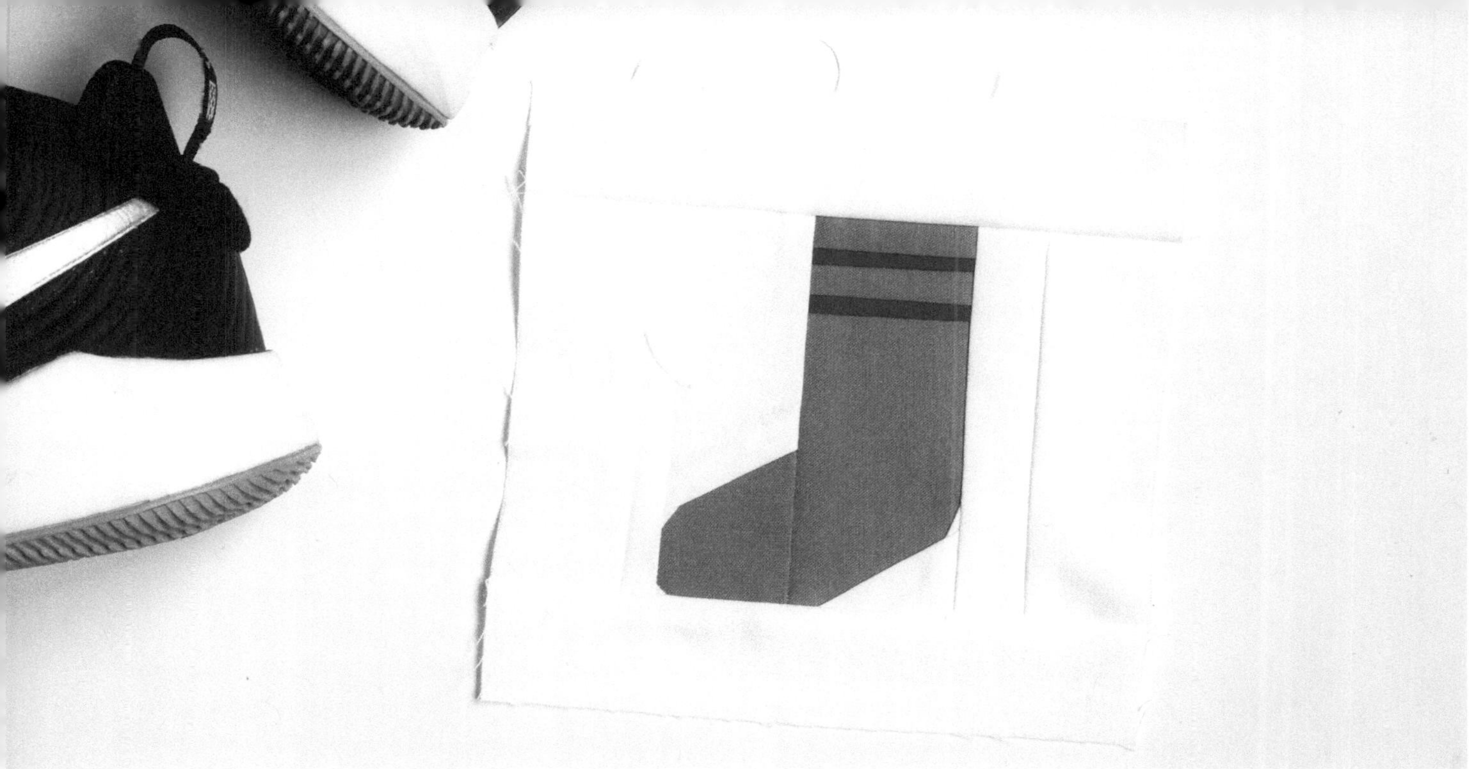

Sock

Fabrics:
Gray
Blue
White

Template: Page 12
Difficulty: Level 1

Section A:
1-Gray
2-White
3-White
4-Blue
5-Gray
6-Blue
7-Gray
8-White

Section B:
1-Gray
2-White
3-White
4-White
5-White

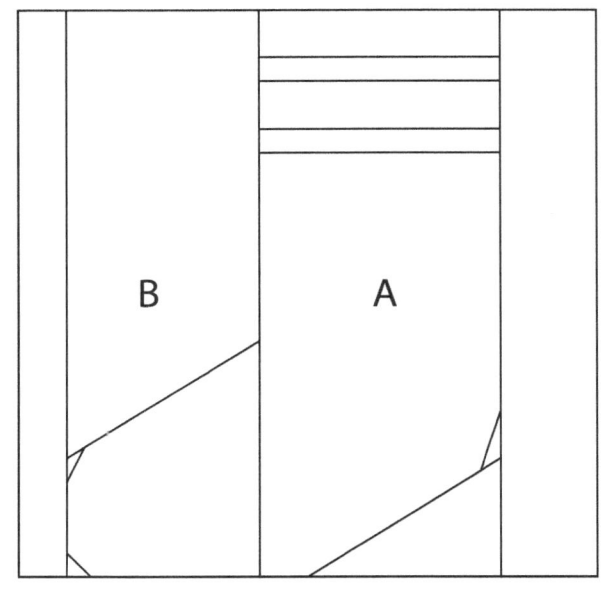

Swimsuit

Fabrics:
Purple
Orange
Pink
Dk Purple
Blue
Green
White

Template: Page 13
Difficulty: Level 1

Section A:

1-White	7-Orange	13-White
2-Purple	8-Pink	14-White
3-Purple	9-Dk Purple	15-White
4-Purple	10-Blue	16-White
5-Purple	11-Green	
6-Purple	12-Purple	

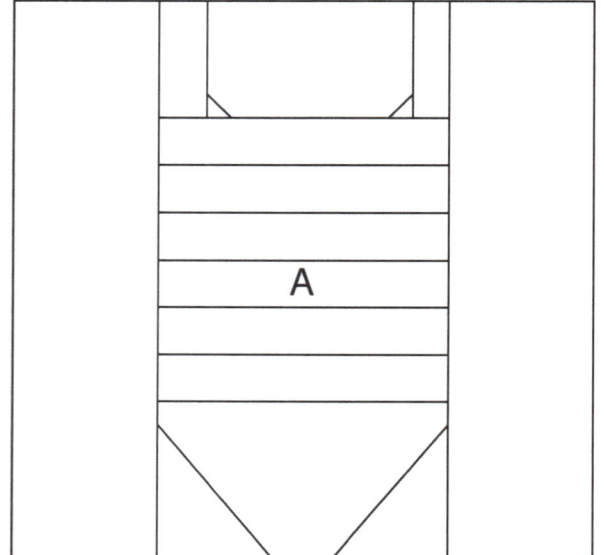

Crown

Fabrics:
Yellow
Red
Blue
White

Template: Page 13
Difficulty: Level 2

Section A:
1-Red   3-Yellow   5-Yellow
2-Yellow   4-Yellow

Section B:
1-Blue   4-Yellow   7-White
2-Yellow   5-Yellow
3-Yellow   6-White

Section C:
1-Blue   4-Yellow   7-White
2-Yellow   5-Yellow
3-Yellow   6-White

Section D:
1-Yellow   2-White

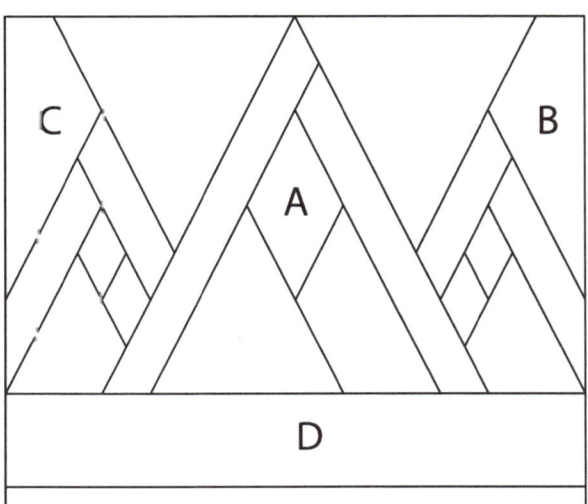

Dress

Fabrics:
Pink
Dk Pink
White

Template: Page 14
Difficulty: Level 2

Section A:
1-White	4-Pink	7-White
2-Pink	5-Pink	8-White
3-Pink	6-Pink	

Section B:
1-Dk Pink	4-Pink	7-White
2-White	5-Dk Pink	
3-White	6-White	

Section C:
1-Dk Pink	2-White	3-White

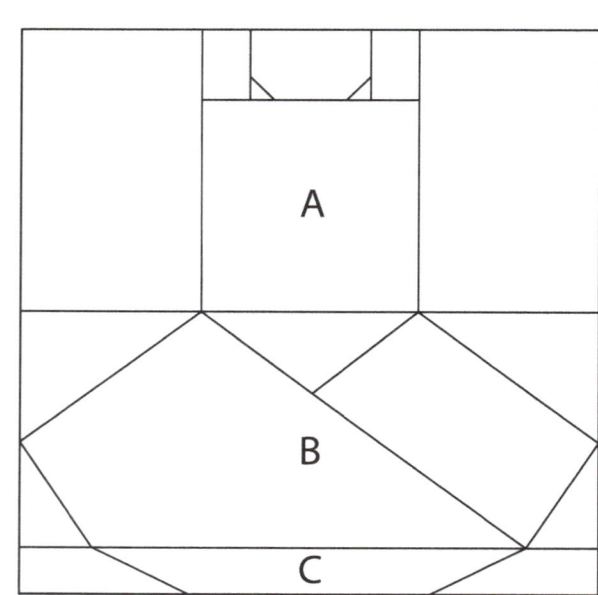

Mitten

Fabrics:
Green
Light Green
White

Template: Page 14
Difficulty: Level 2

Section A:
1-Green
2-White
3-White
4-Lt Green
5-Green
6-Lt Green
7-Green
8-White
9-White
10-White

Section B:
1-Green
2-White
3-White

Section C:
1-Green
2-White
3-White
4-White
5-White

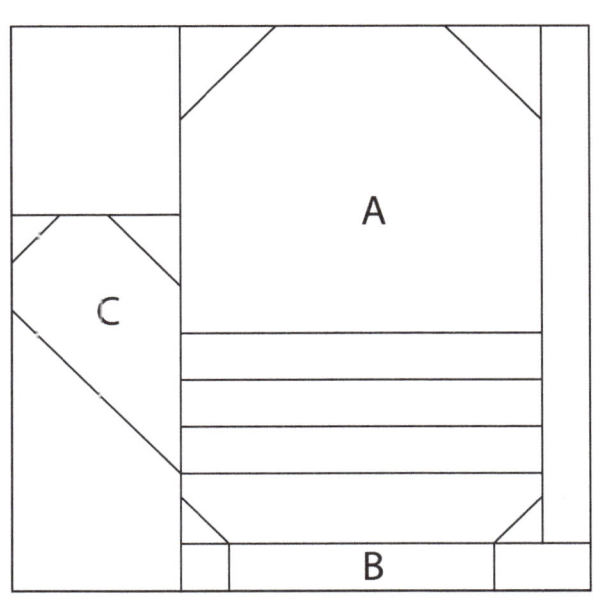

Shirt

Fabrics:
Purple
White

Template: Page 15
Difficulty: Level 1

Section A:
1-White
2-Purple
3-Purple
4-White
5-White
6-Purple

Section B:
1-Purple
2-White
3-White

Snow Boot

x — x — x — x

Fabrics:
Dark Blue
Blue
Dark Gray
White

Template: Page 15
Difficulty: Level 2

Section A:
1-Dk Blue   4-Blue   7-Dk Blue
2-Blue   5-Blue   8-White
3-Dk Blue   6-Blue   9-White

Section B:
1-Blue   3-Dk Gray   5-White
2-White   4-White

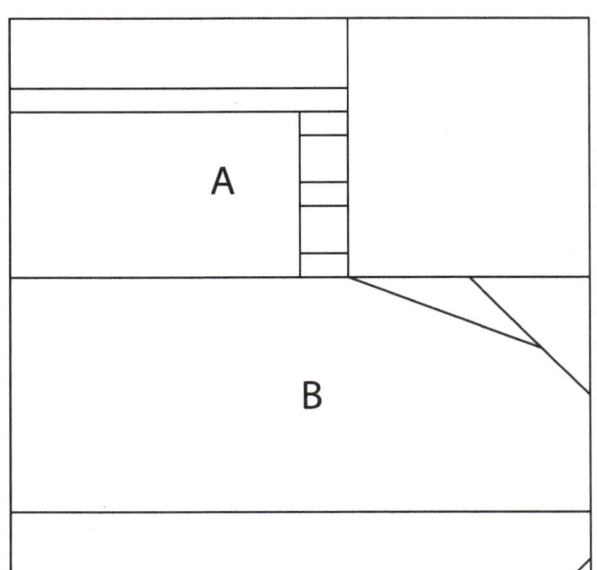

Bunny

Fabrics:
Light Gray
Pink
White

Template: Page 16
Difficulty: Level 1

Section A:
1-White
2-Lt Gray
3-Lt Gray
4-Pink
5-Pink
6-Lt Gray
7-Lt Gray
8-White
9-White

Section B:
1-Lt Gray
2-White
3-Pink
4-Lt Gray
5-White
6-Lt Gray
7-White
8-White

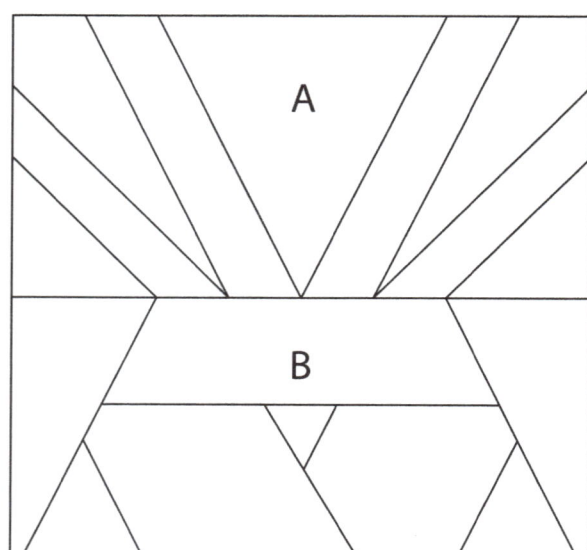

Cat

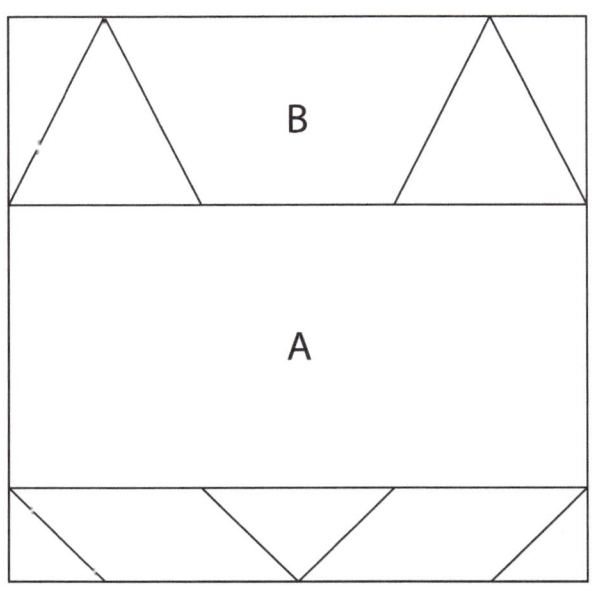

Fabrics:
Orange
Light Pink
White

Template: Page 16
Difficulty: Level 1

Section A:
1-Lt Pink
2-Orange
3-Orange
4-White
5-White
6-Orange

Section B:
1-White
2-Orange
3-Orange
4-White
5-White

Puppy

Fabrics:
Brown
Dark Brown
Tan
White

Template: Page 17
Difficulty: Level 3

Section A:
1-White   2-Brown

Section B:
1-Brown   3-Dk Brown   5-White
2-Dk Brown   4-White   6-White

Section C:
1-Brown   3-Dk Brown   5-White
2-Dk Brown   4-White   6-White

Section D:
1-Dk Brown   6-Tan   11-Brown
2-Tan   7-Brown   12-White
3-Tan   8-Brown   13-White
4-Tan   9-Brown   14-White
5-Tan   10-Brown   15-White

Section E:
1-Tan   3-White   4-White
2-White

Chicken

Fabrics:
Light Brown
Red
Yellow
White

Template: Page 17
Difficulty: Level 2

Section A:
1-Lt Brown   4-White   7-White
2-White   5-Lt Brown   8-White
3-White   6-Lt Brown

Section B:
1-Yellow   2-White   3-White

Section C:
1-White   3-White   5-White
2-Red   4-White

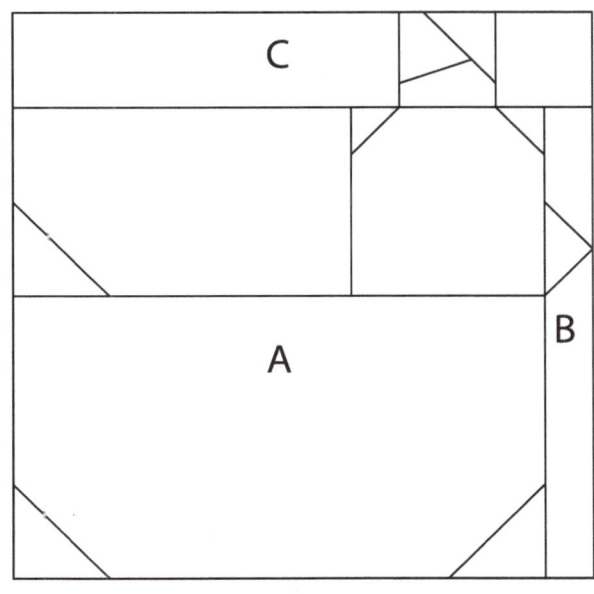

Fish

Fabrics:
Orange
White

Template: Page 18
Difficulty: Level 1

Section A:
1-Orange   2-White   3-White

Section B:
1-Orange   2-White   3-White

Section C:
1-Orange   2-White   3-White

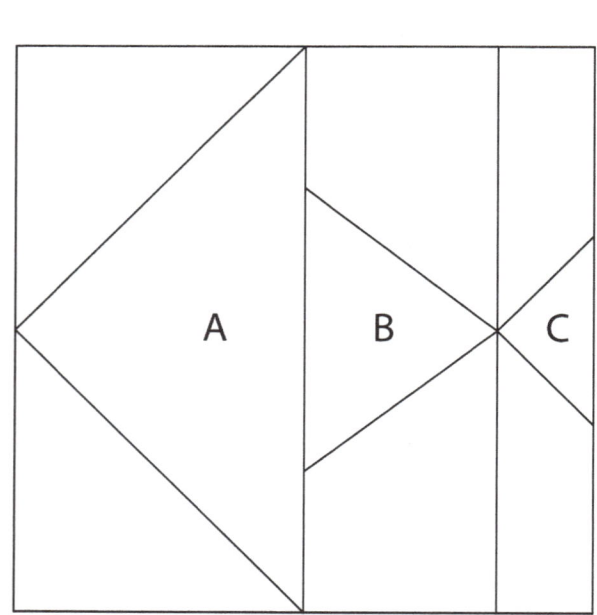

Cow

Fabrics:
Brown
Dark Brown
Lt Pink
Black
Tan
White

Template: Page 18
Difficulty: Level 3

Section A:
1-Lt Pink	5-Lt Pink	9-Brown
2-Black	6-Lt Pink	10-Brown
3-Black	7-Lt Pink	11-Brown
4-Lt Pink	8-Brown	12-Brown

Section B:
1-Brown   2-White   3-White

Section C:
1-Brown   2-White   3-White

Section D:
1-Brown	4-White	6-White
2-Dk Brown	5-White	7-White
3-Dk Brown		

Section E:
1-White	3-Tan	5-White
2-Tan	4-White	

Dolphin

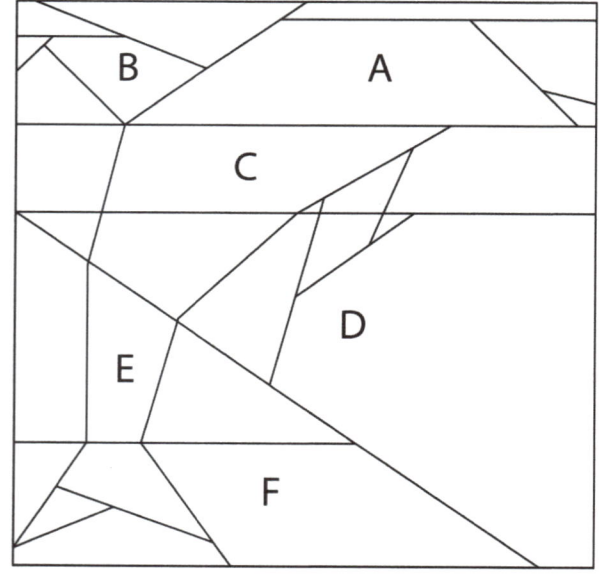

Fabrics:
Blue
White

Template: Page 19
Difficulty: Level 3

Note: Sew E to F before sewing to ABCD

Section A:
1-White
2-Blue
3-Blue
4-White

Section B:
1-Blue
2-White
3-White
4-White
5-White

Section C:
1-Blue
2-White
3-White
4-Blue
5-White

Section D:
1-Blue
2-White
3-White
4-White
5-Blue
6-White

Section E:
1-Blue
2-White
3-White

Section F:
1-Blue
2-White
3-Blue
4-White
5-White

Duck

o-o-o-o-o-o

Fabrics:
Yellow
Orange
White

Template: Page 19
Difficulty: Level 2

Section A:
1-Yellow   3-White   5-White
2-White   4-White

Section B:
1-White   2-Yellow   3-White

Section C:
1-Orange   2-White   3-White

Section D:
1-Yellow   3-White   5-White
2-White   4-White

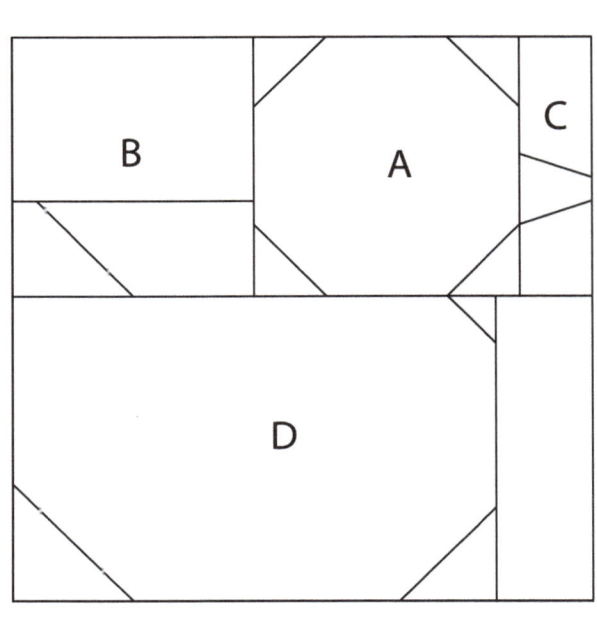

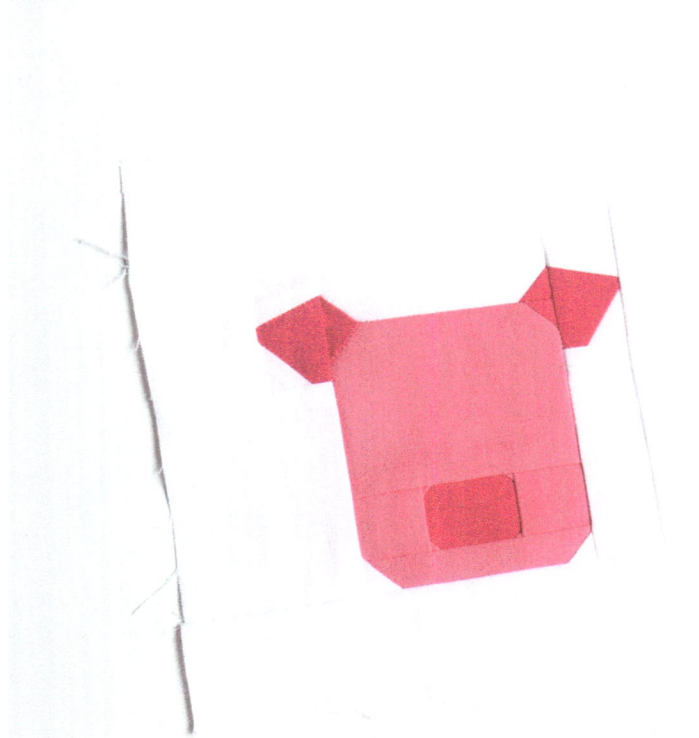

Pig
~~~~~~~~~~

Fabrics:
Light Pink
PInk
White

Template: Page 20
Difficulty: Level 2

Section A:
1-Pink	6-Lt Pink	11-Lt Pink
2-Lt Pink	7-Lt Pink	12-Pink
3-Lt Pink	8-Lt Pink	13-Pink
4-Lt Pink	9-White	
5-Lt Pink	10-White	

Section B:
1-White 2-Pink 3-Pink

Section C:
1-Pink 3-White 4-White
2-White

Section D:
1-Pink 3-White 4-White
2-White

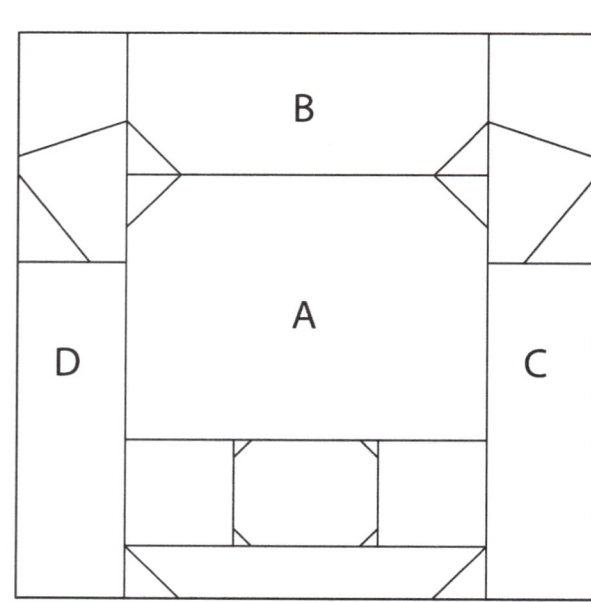

Narwhal

Fabrics:
Blue
Tan
White

Template: Page 20
Difficulty: Level 1

Section A:
1-White
2-Blue
3-White
4-Blue
5-Blue
6-White
7-White
8-White

Section B:
1-Tan
2-White
3-White

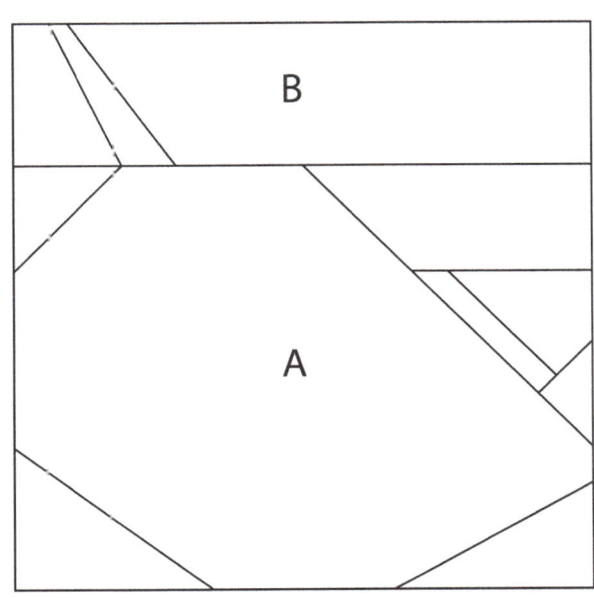

Monkey

Fabrics:
Brown
Pink
Tan
White

Template: Page 21
Difficulty: Level 2

Section A:
1-Tan	5-Tan	9-Brown
2-Brown	6-White	10-White
3-White	7-Brown	11-White
4-Pink	8-White	12-White

Section B:
1-Tan	4-White	6-White
2-White	5-White	7-White
3-White		

Section C:
1-Tan	4-White	6-White
2-White	5-White	7-White
3-White		

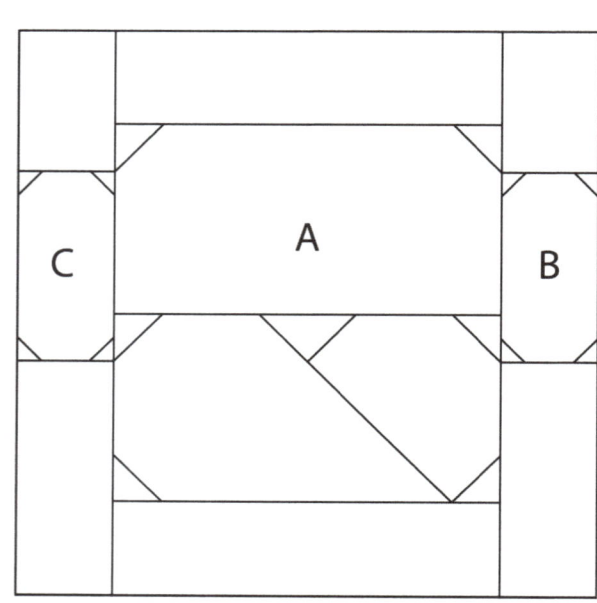

Mouse

Fabrics:
Light Gray
Light Pink
White

Template: Page 21
Difficulty: Level 2

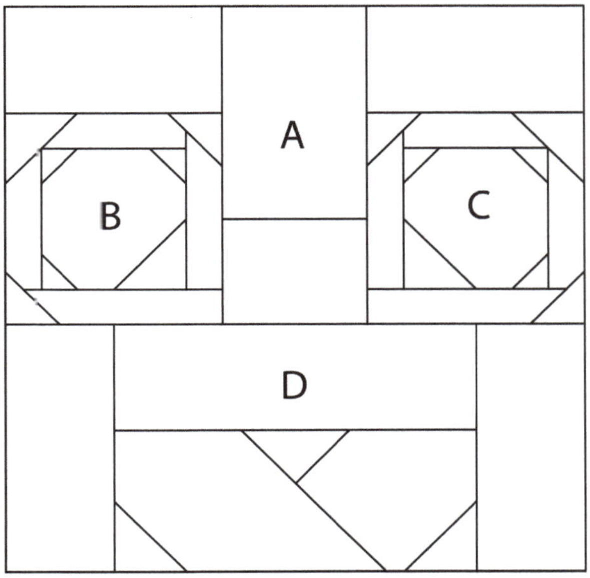

Section A:
1-White 2-Lt Gray

Section B:
1-Lt Pink   6-Lt Gray   11-White
2-Lt Gray   7-Lt Gray   12-White
3-Lt Gray   8-Lt Gray   13-White
4-Lt Gray   9-Lt Gray
5-Lt Gray   10-White

Section C:
1-Lt Pink   6-Lt Gray   11-White
2-Lt Gray   7-Lt Gray   12-White
3-Lt Gray   8-Lt Gray   13-White
4-Lt Gray   9-Lt Gray
5-Lt Gray   10-White

Section D:
1-Lt Gray   4-Lt Gray   7-White
2-White   5-White   8-White
3-Lt Pink   6-Lt Gray

Candy Corn

Fabrics:
Light Cream
Yellow
Orange
White

Template: Page 22
Difficulty: Level 1

Section A:
1-Orange
2-White
3-White
4-Yellow
5-Lt Cream
6-White
7-White
8-White
9-White
10-White

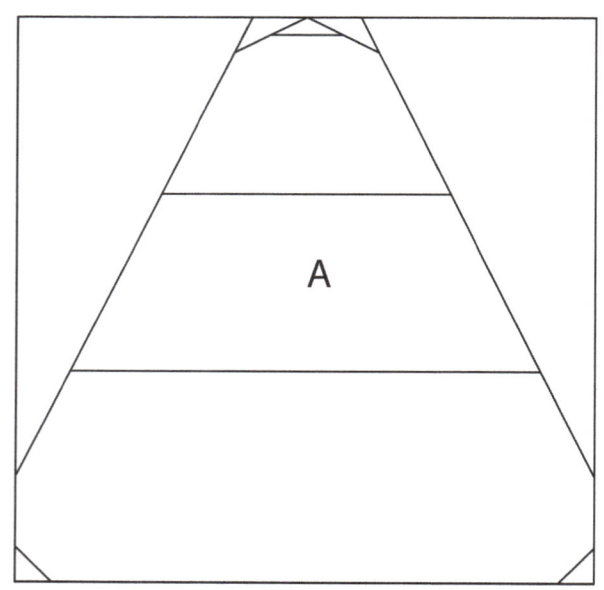

Balloon

Fabrics:
Pink
Light Gray
White

Template: Page 22
Difficulty: Level 2

Section A:
1-Pink	4-White	7-White
2-White	5-White	
3-White	6-White	

Section B:
1-Pink   2-White   3-White

Section C:
1-Lt Gray   2-White   3-White

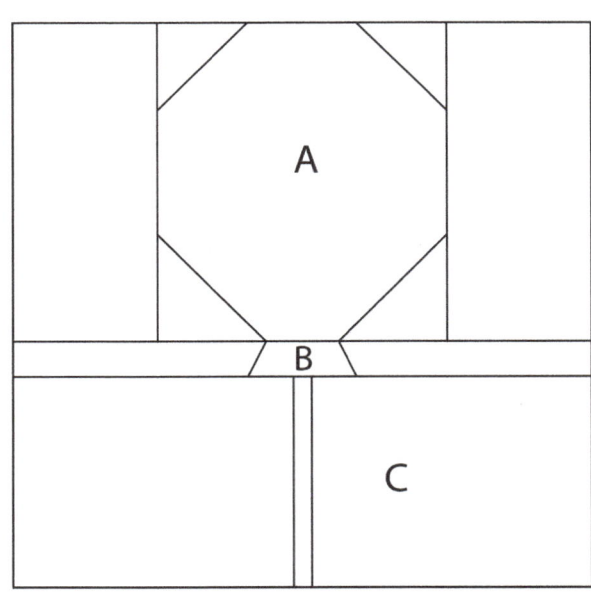

Witch Hat

Fabrics:
Black
Purple
White

Template: Page 23
Difficulty: Level 1

Section A:
1-Purple
2-Black
3-White
4-White
5-Black

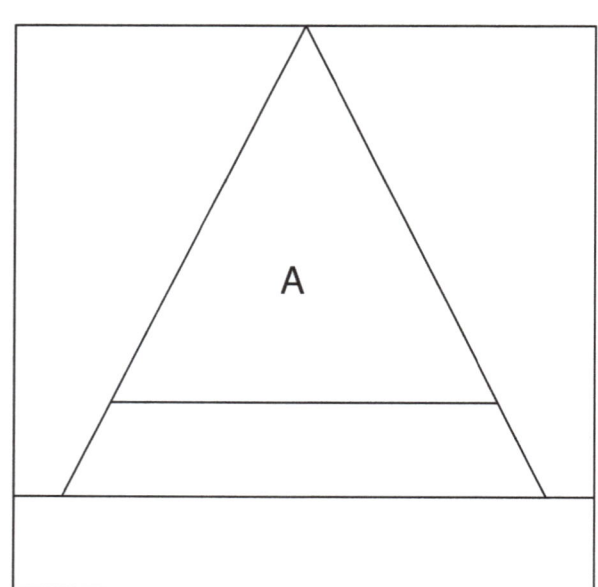

Christmas Light

oxoxoxox

Fabrics:
Green
Gray
Dark Gray
White

Template: Page 23
Difficulty: Level 2

Section A:
1-Green
2-White
3-White
4-White
5-White
6-White
7-White
8-White

Section B:
1-Dk Gray
2-Gray
3-Gray
4-Dk Gray
5-Gray
6-White
7-White
8-White

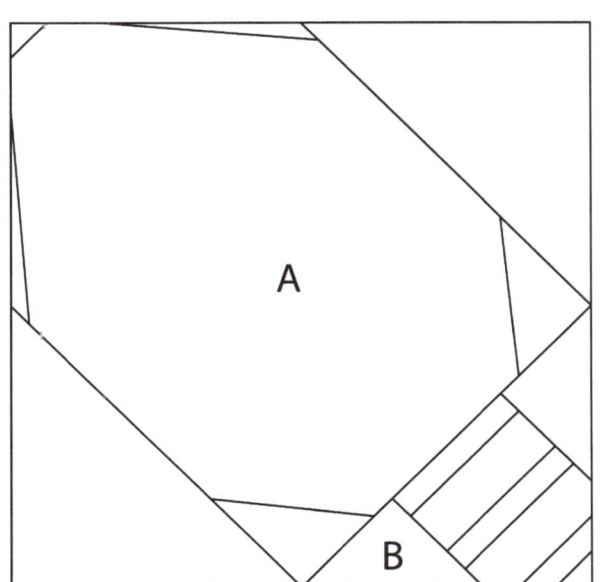

Cupcake

Fabrics:
Yellow
Blue
Pink
Teal
Dark Teal
White

Template: Page 24
Difficulty: Level 2

Section A:
1-Yellow	4-White	7-White
2-White	5-White	
3-White	6-White	

Section B:
1-Blue   2-White   3-White

Section C:
1-Pink	3-White	5-White
2-White	4-White	

Section D:
1-Dk Teal	4-Dk Teal	7-White
2-Teal	5-Dk Teal	
3-Teal	6-White	

56

Easter Egg

Fabrics:
Green
Yellow
Pink
White

Template: Page 24
Difficulty: Level 1

Section A:
1-Green
2-Yellow
3-Pink
4-Pink
5-White
6-White
7-White
8-White
9-White
10-White
11-White
12-White
13-White
14-White

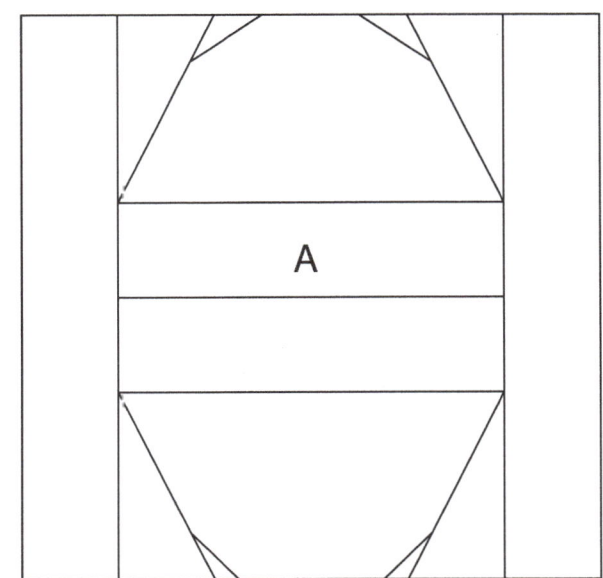

Ghost

— . — . — . — . —

Fabrics:
Light Gray
Black
White

Template: Page 25
Difficulty: Level 1

Section A:
1-Lt Gray
2-Black
3-Black
4-Lt Gray
5-Lt Gray
6-Lt Gray
7-White
8-White
9-Lt Gray
10-White
11-White

Section B:
1-White
2-Lt Gray
3-Lt Gray
4-White
5-White
6-Lt Gray
7-Lt Gray
8-White
9-White

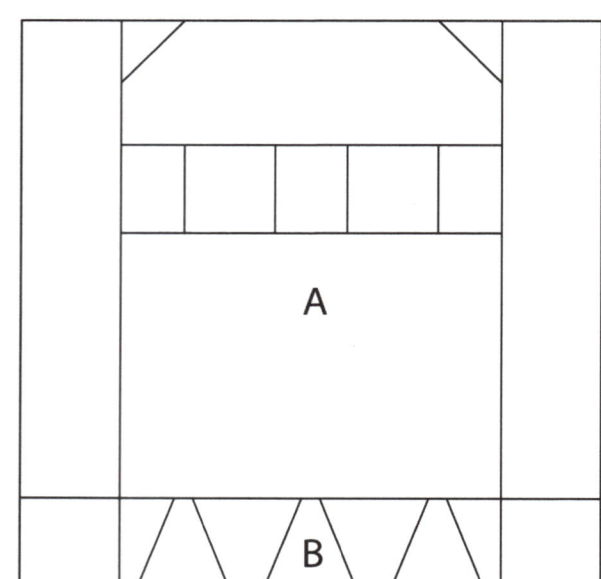

Firecracker

Fabrics:
Red
Blue
Light Gray
Dark Gray
White

Template: Page 25
Difficulty: Level 1

Section A:
1-Red	5-Lt Gray	9-White
2-Lt Gray	6-Red	10-Red
3-Blue	7-Blue	
4-Blue	8-White	

Section B:
1-Dk Gray	2-White	3-White

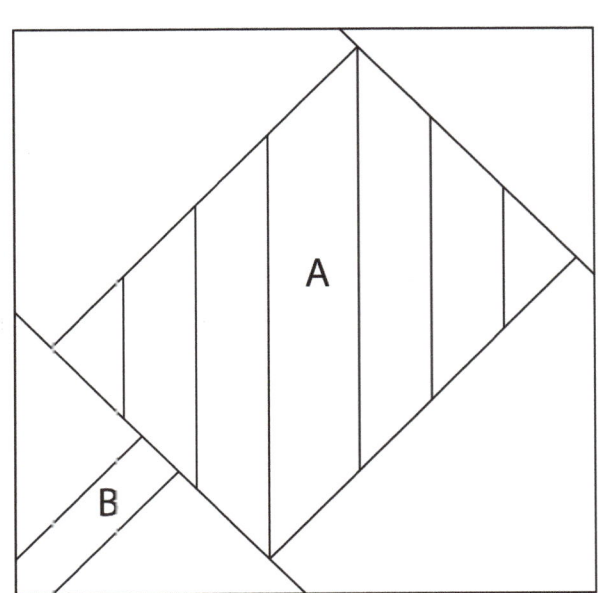

Flag

Fabrics:
Red
Blue
White

Template: Page 26
Difficulty: Level 1

Section A:
1-White
2-Red
3-Red
4-Blue
5-White
6-Red
7-White
8-Red
9-White

Heart

Fabrics:
Pink
White

Template: Page 26
Difficulty: Level 1

Section A:
1-Pink
2-White
3-White
4-Pink
5-White
6-White
7-White

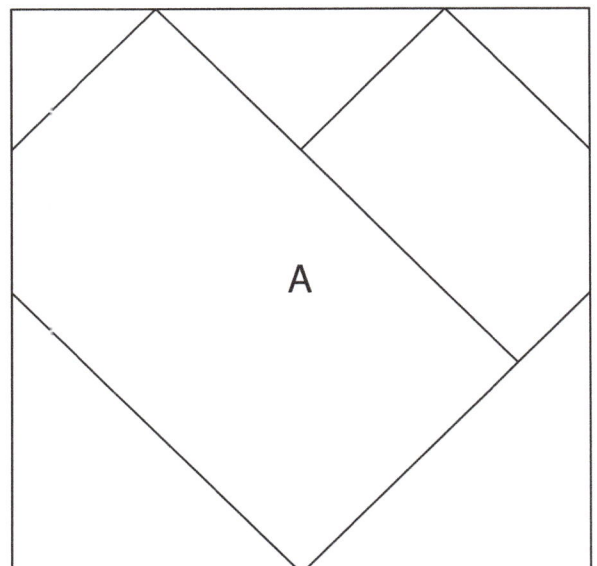

Present

Fabrics:
Green
Red
White

Template: Page 27
Difficulty: Level 1

Section A:
1-White   3-Green   5-White
2-Green   4-White

Section B:
1-Green   2-Red   3-Red

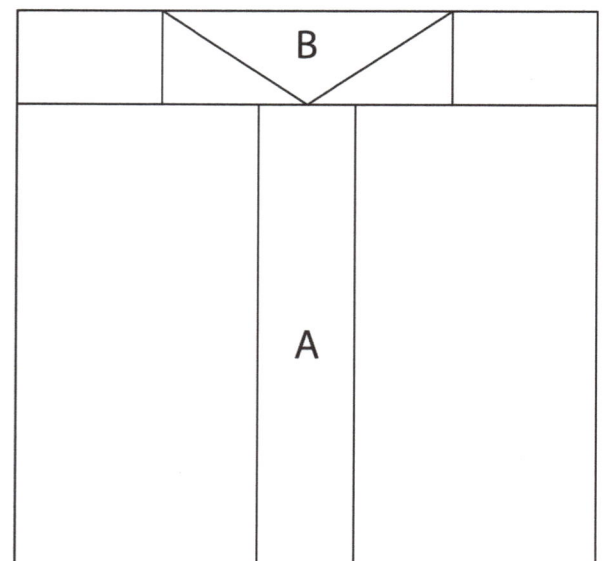

Pumpkin

Fabrics:
Orange
Green
White

Template: Page 27
Difficulty: Level 1

Section A:
1-Orange   3-White   5-White
2-White   4-White

Section B:
1-Green   3-White   4-White
2-White

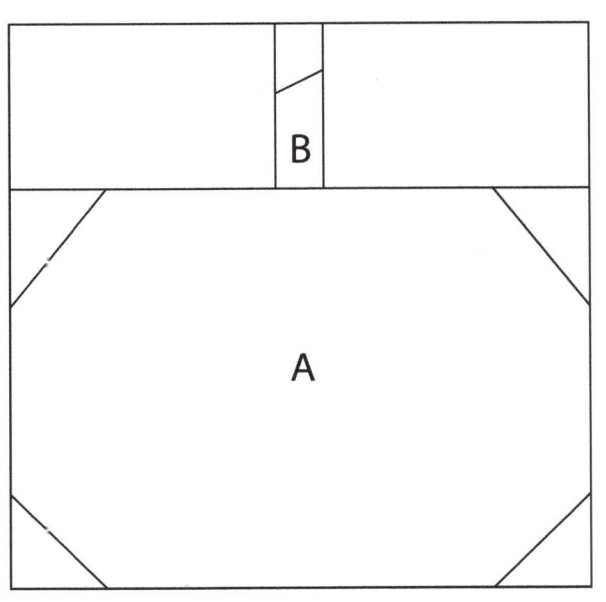

Santa Hat

Fabrics:
Red
Light Cream
White

Template: Page 28
Difficulty: Level 2

Section A:
1-Lt Cream	4-White	7-White
2-White	5-White	
3-White	6-White	

Section B:
1-Red	2-White	3-White

Section C:
1-Lt Cream	3-White	5-White
2-White	4-White	

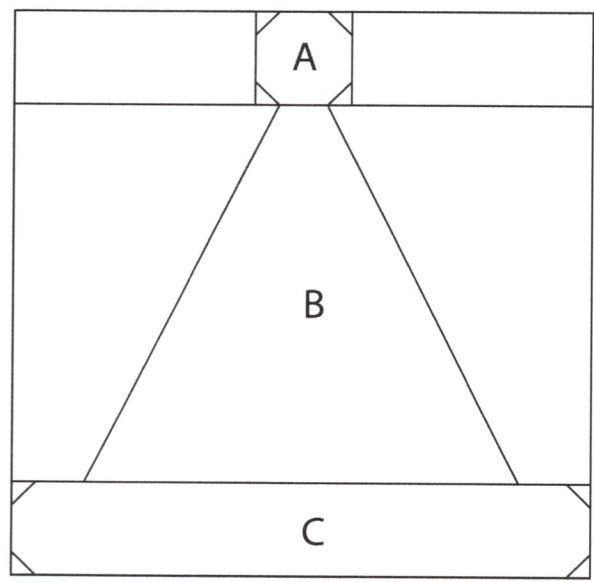

Star

Fabrics:
Yellow
White

Template: Page 28
Difficulty: Level 2

Section A:
1-White   3-Yellow   5-White
2-Yellow   4-White

Section B:
1-Yellow   3-White   5-White
2-White   4-White

Section C:
1-Yellow   2-White   3-White

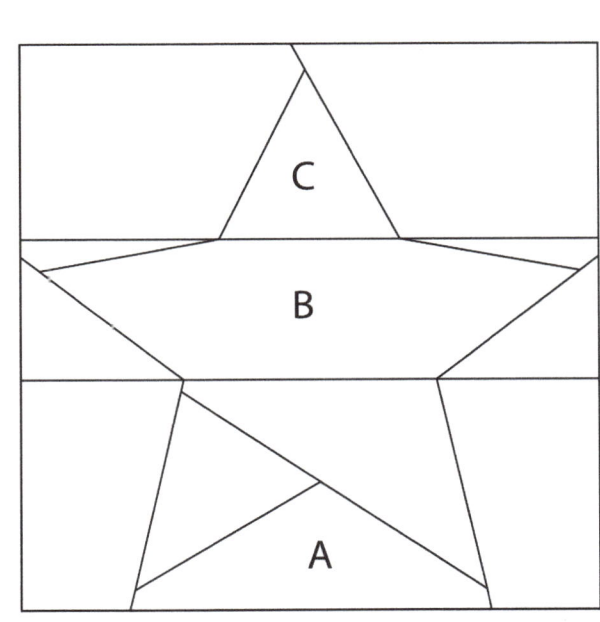

Tulip

Fabrics:
Pink
Green
White

Template: Page 29
Difficulty: Level 1

Section A:
1-Pink	5-Pink	8-White
2-White	6-Pink	9-White
3-Pink	7-White	10-White
4-White		

Section B:
1-Green	3-White	5-Green
2-White	4-White	6-White

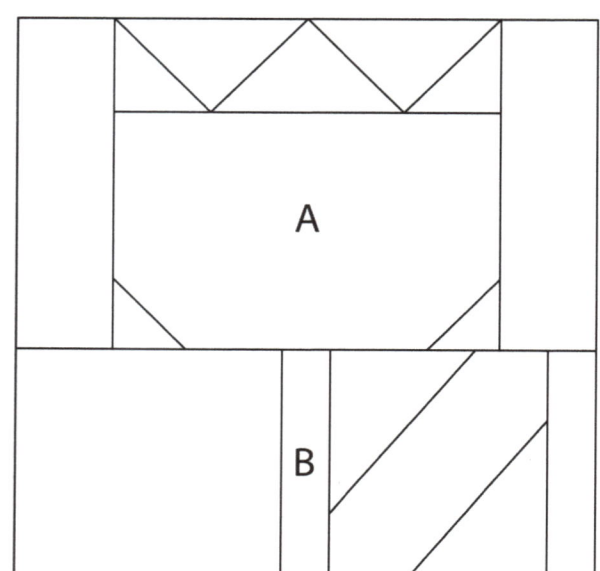

Watering Can

Fabrics:
Green
White

Template: Page 29
Difficulty: Level 2

Section A:
1-White   2-Green   3-White

Section B:
1-Green   3-Green   4-White
2-White

Section C:
1-White   5-White   9-White
2-Green   6-Green   10-White
3-Green   7-Green   11-Green
4-Green   8-White

Section D:
1-Green   3-White   4-White
2-White

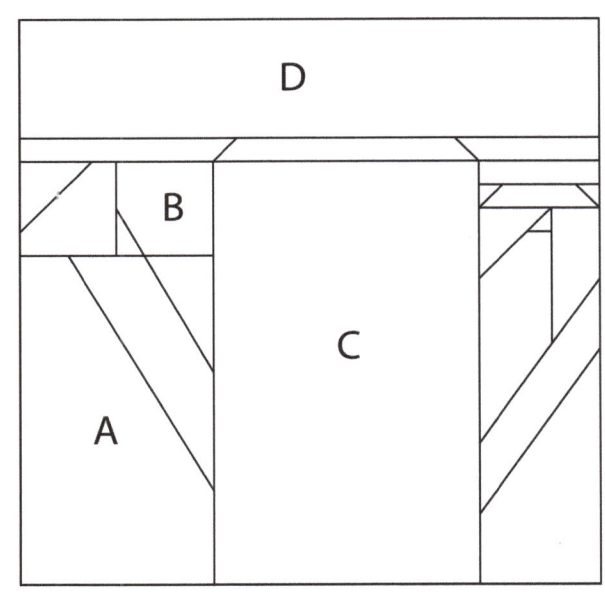

Tree

Fabrics:
Green
Brown
White

Template: Page 30
Difficulty: Level 1

Section A:
1-Green   3-White   5-White
2-White   4-White

Section B:
1-Brown   2-White   3-White

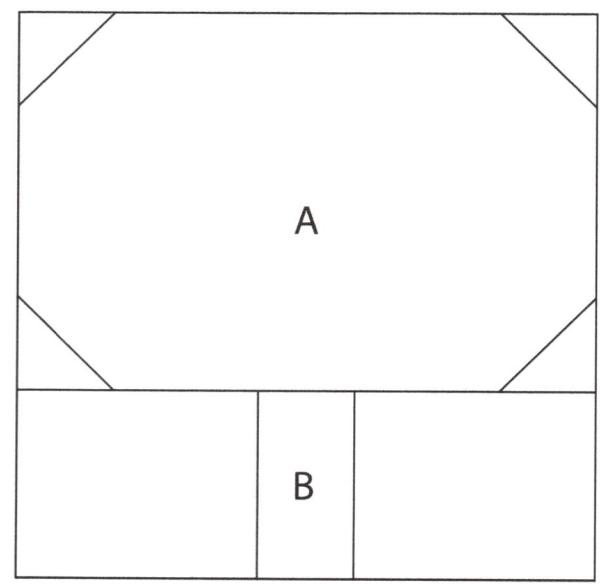

Fire Hydrant

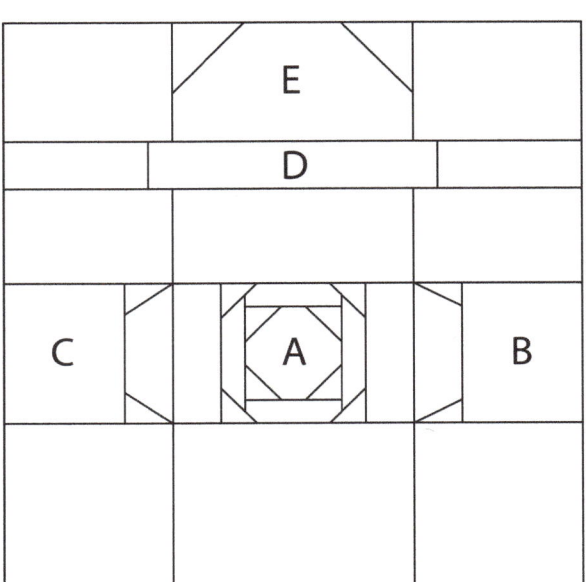

Fabrics:
Red
Light Red
Dark Red
White

Template: Page 30
Difficulty: Level 3

Section A:
1-Lt Red
2-Dk Red
3-Dk Red
4-Dk Red
5-Dk Red
6-Dk Red
7-Dk Red
8-Dk Red
9-Dk Red
10-Red
11-Red
12-Red
13-Red
14-Red
15-Red
16-Red
17-Red

Section B:
1-Dk Red
2-White
3-White
4-White
5-White
6-White

Section C:
1-Dk Red
2-White
3-White
4-White
5-White
6-White

Section D:
1-Dk Red
2-White
3-White

Section E:
1-White
2-Red
3-White
4-White
5-White

Butterfly

Fabrics:	**Template: Page 31**
Brown	**Difficulty: Level 2**
Blue	
Light Blue	
White	

Section A:
1-Brown	3-White	5-White
2-White	4-White	

Section B:
1-Lt Blue	4-White	6-White
2-White	5-White	7-White
3-Dk Blue		

Section C:
1-Lt Blue	4-White	6-White
2-White	5-White	7-White
3-Dk Blue		

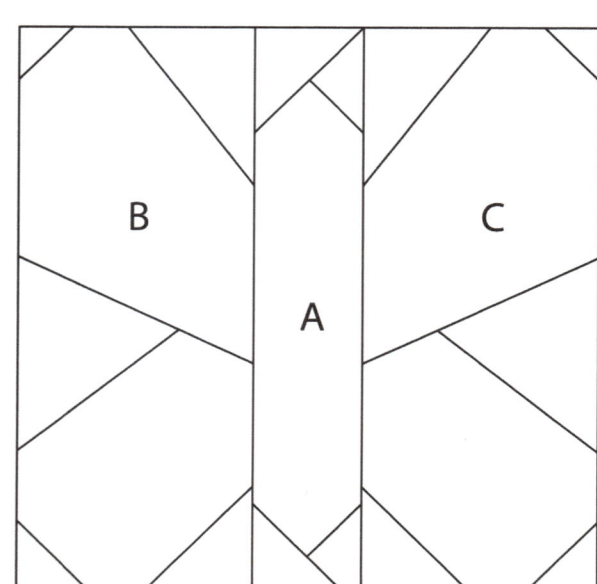

Leaf

o x o x o x o x

Fabrics:
Green
Dark Green
White

Template: Page 31
Difficulty: Level 1

Section A:
1-Dk Green	4-White	6-White
2-Green	5-White	7-White
3-Green		

Section B:
| 1-Dk Green | 2-White | 3-White |

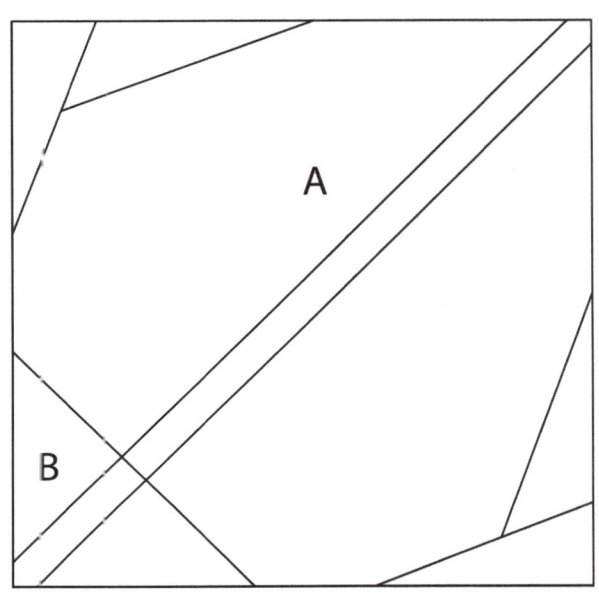

Cactus

Fabrics:
Green
White

Template: Page 32
Difficulty: Level 2

Section A:
1-Green   2-White   3-White

Section B:
1-Green   4-White   7-White
2-White   5-White   8-White
3-White   6-Green

Section C:
1-Green   4-White   7-White
2-White   5-White   8-White
3-White   6-Green

Flower

Fabrics:
Purple
Yellow
White

Template: Page 32
Difficulty: Level 3

Section A:
1-Yellow
2-Purple
3-Purple
4-Purple
5-White
6-White
7-White
8-White

Section B:
1-Yellow
2-Purple
3-Purple
4-Purple
5-White
6-White
7-White
8-White

Section C:
1-Yellow
2-Purple
3-Purple
4-Purple
5-White
6-White
7-White
8-White

Section D:
1-Yellow
2-Purple
3-Purple
4-Purple
5-White
6-White
7-White
8-White

Note: Sew A to B and C to D, then combine.

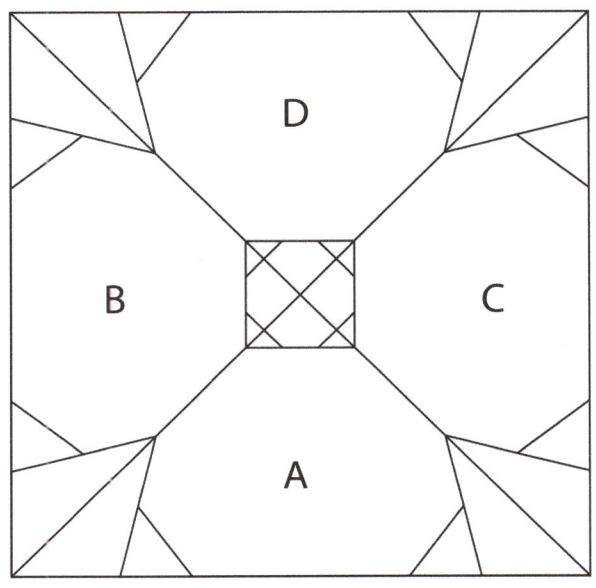

Toadstool

Fabrics:
Red
Tan
White

Template: Page 33
Difficulty: Level 1

Section A:
1-Tan
2-White
3-White
4-Red
5-White
6-White

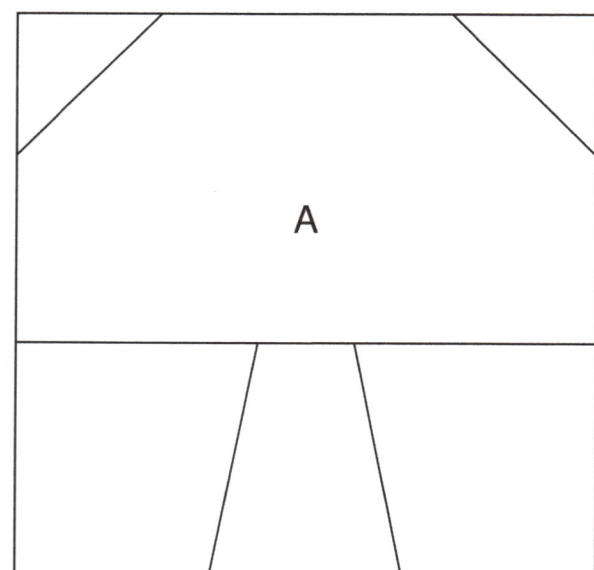

Mail Box

Fabrics:
Light Gray
Gray
Brown
Red
White

Template: Page 33
Difficulty: Level 2

Section A:
1-Red
2-Lt Gray
3-Lt Gray
4-White
5-White

Section B:
1-Red
2-White
3-Red
4-White

Section C:
1-Gray
2-White
3-Lt Gray
4-White
5-Lt Gray
6-White

Section D:
1-Brown
2-White
3-White

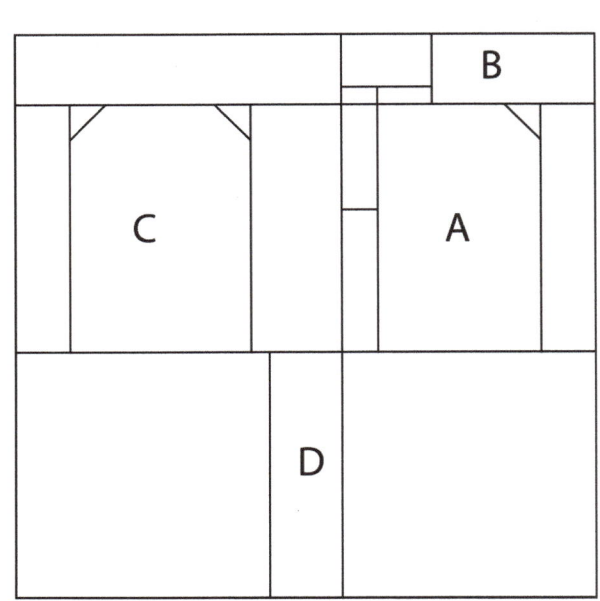

Inchworm

Fabrics:
Light Green
Bright Green
White

Template: Page 34
Difficulty: Level 3

Section A:
1-Lt Green
2-White
3-White
4-Brt Green
5-Brt Green
6-Brt Green
7-White
8-Brt Green
9-White
10-White

Section B:
1-Brt Green
2-White
3-White
4-White
5-Brt Green
6-White

Section C:
1-White
2-Brt Green
3-White
4-Brt Green
5-White
6-Brt Green
7-White
8-Brt Green
9-White
10-Brt Green
11-White

Section D:
1-Brt Green
2-White
3-White
4-White
5-White
6-White

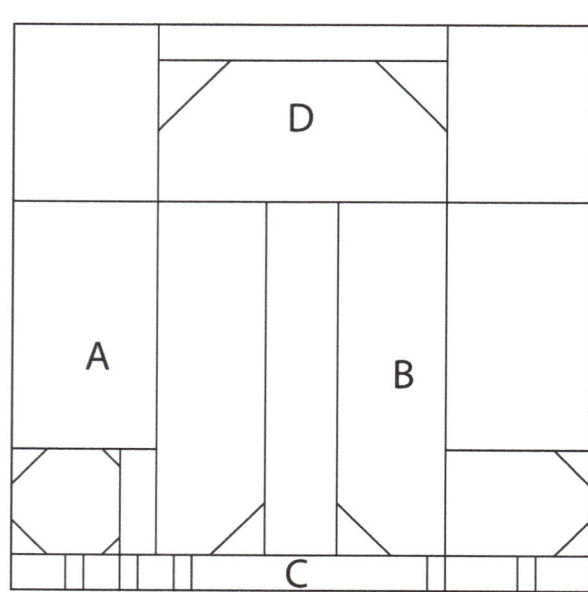

Ladybug

Fabrics:
Red
Black
White

Template: Page 35
Difficulty: Level 2

Section A:
1-Black	5-Red	9-Red
2-Red	6-Red	10-White
3-Red	7-Red	11-Black
4-Red	8-Red	12-White

Section B:
1-Black	5-Red	9-Red
2-Red	6-Red	10-White
3-Red	7-Red	11-White
4-Red	8-Red	

Section C:
1-Black	3-White	4-White
2-White		

Section C:
1-White

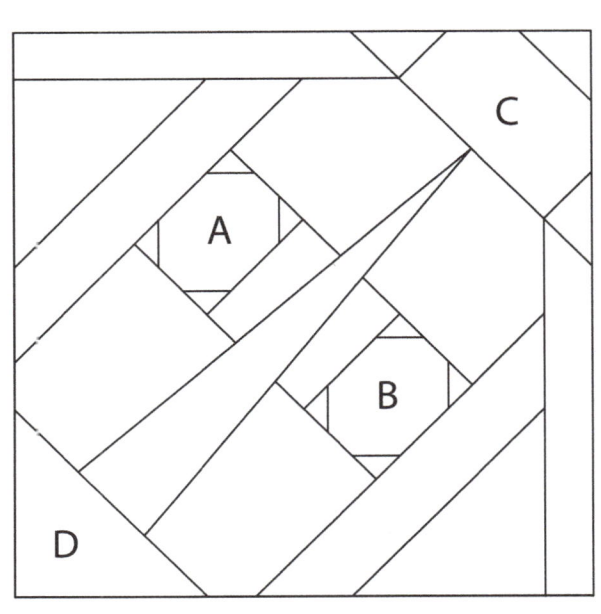

Pine Tree

Fabrics:
Green
Brown
White

Template: Page 35
Difficulty: Level 1

Section A:
1-Green   2-White   3-White

Section B:
1-Brown   2-White   3-White

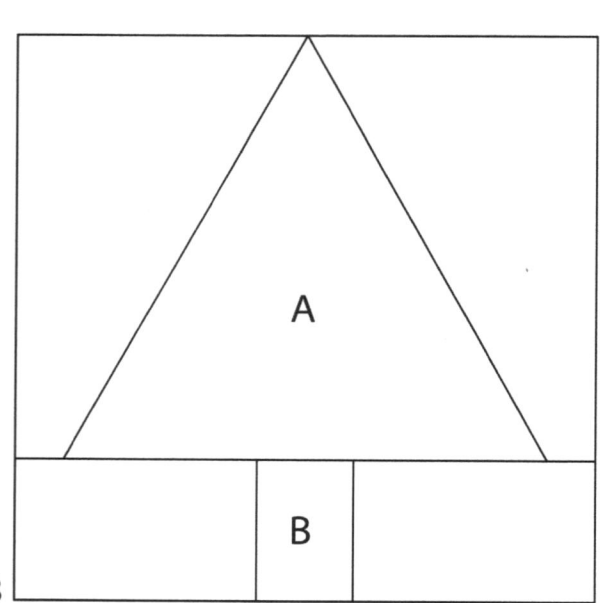

Train

Fabrics:
Gray
Red
Black
White

Template: Page 36
Difficulty: Level 3

Section A:
1-Gray	3-White	4-White
2-White		

Section B:
1-White	4-Red	7-White
2-Red	5-Red	8-Gray
3-Red	6-White	

Section C:
1-Black	4-Red	6-Red
2-Red	5-Red	7-White
3-Red		

Section D:
1-Black	3-Red	4-Red
2-Red		

Section E:
1-Black	3-White	4-White
2-White		

Section F:
1-Black	3-White	4-White
2-White		

Section G:
1-Red	2-White	3-White

Note: Sew AB, CD and EF together in rows follow ng diagram below, combine CD and EF, then add G and sew to AB

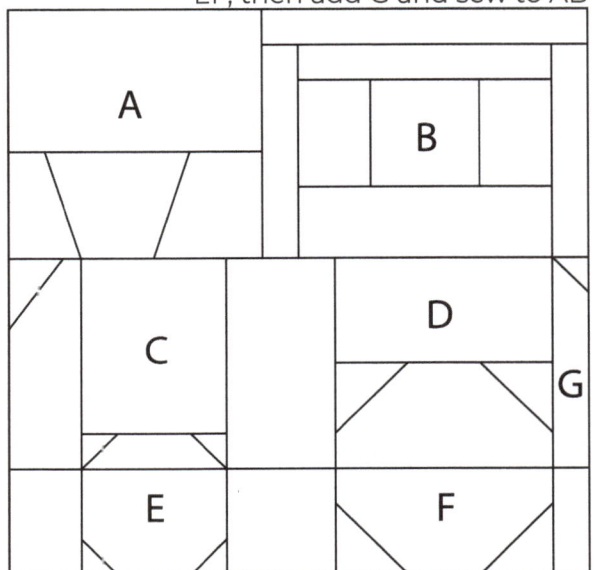

Boat

Fabrics:
Brown
Blue
White

Template: Page 36
Difficulty: Level 1

Section A:
1-Blue
2-White
3-White
4-Brown
5-White
6-Brown
7-White
8-White

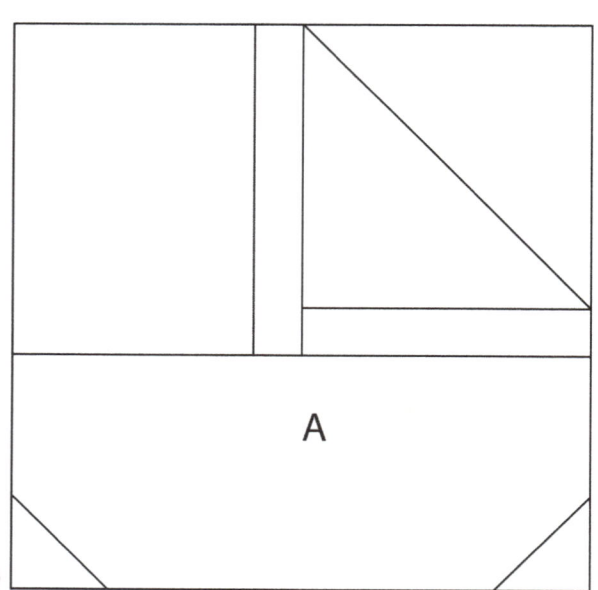

School Bus

Fabrics:
Yellow
Black
Light Gray
White

Template: Page 37
Difficulty: Level 2

Section A:
1-Black
2-White
3-White
4-White

Section B:
1-Black
2-White
3-White
4-White
5-White

Section C:
1-Yellow
2-Lt Gray
3-Yellow
4-Lt Gray
5-Yellow
6-Lt Gray
7-Yellow
8-Lt Gray
9-Yellow
10-Yellow
11-Yellow
12-White
13-White
14-White

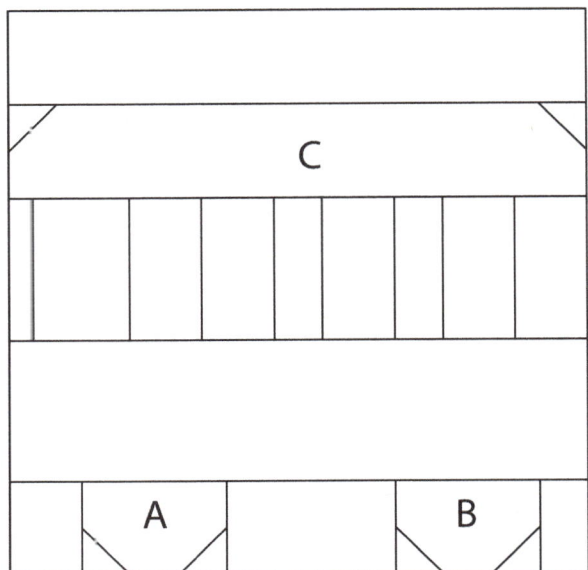

Truck

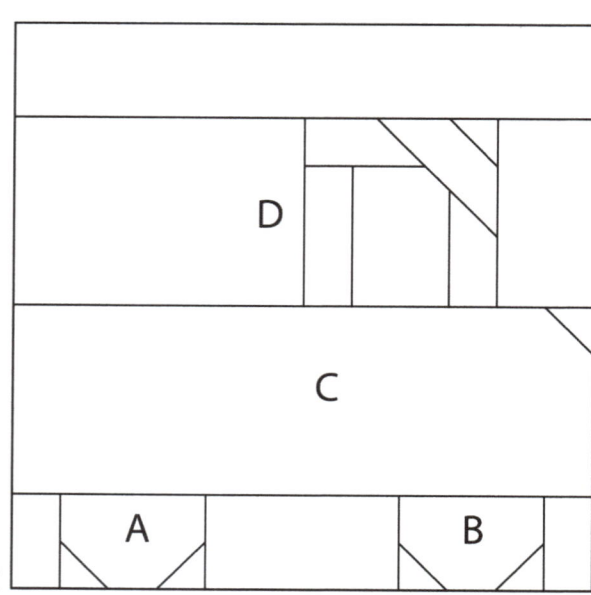

Fabrics:
Red
Light Gray
Black
White

Template: Page 37
Difficulty: Level 2

Section A:
1-Black
2-White
3-White
4-White

Section B:
1-Black
2-White
3-White
4-White
5-White

Section C:
1-Red
2-White

Section D:
1-Lt Gray
2-Red
3-Red
4-Red
5-Red
6-White
7-White
8-White
9-White

Airplane

Fabrics:
Gray
White

Template: Page 38
Difficulty: Level 2

Section A:
1-Gray
2-White
3-White
4-White
5-Gray
6-Gray
7-White

Section B:
1-Gray
2-White
3-White
4-White
5-Gray

Section C:
1-White

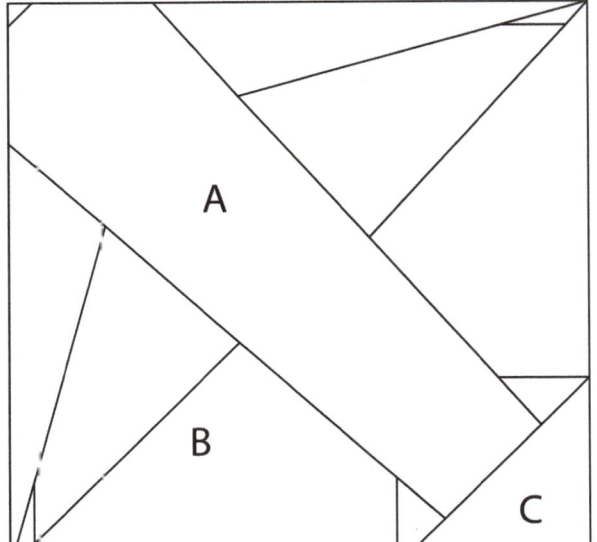

Car

Fabrics:
Blue
Light Gray
Black
White

Template: Page 38
Difficulty: Level 2

Section A:
1-Black
2-White
3-White
4-White
5-White

Section B:
1-Black
2-White
3-White
4-White

Section C:
1-Blue
2-White
3-White

Section D:
1-Blue
2-Lt Gray
3-Blue
4-Blue
5-White
6-White
7-White
8-White
9-White

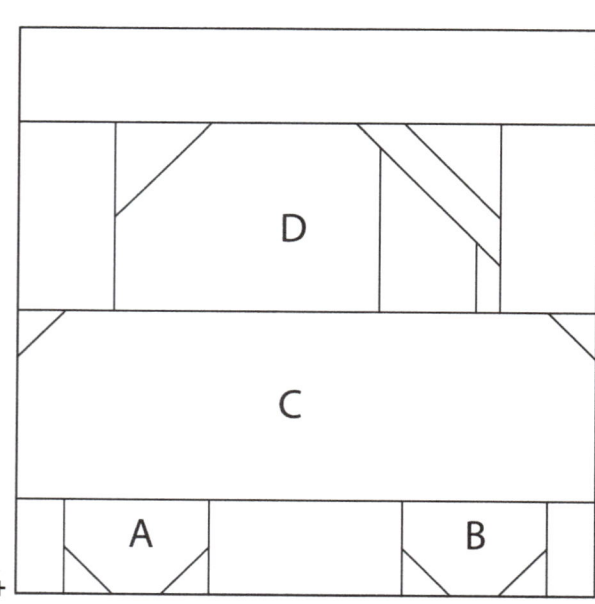

Space Shuttle

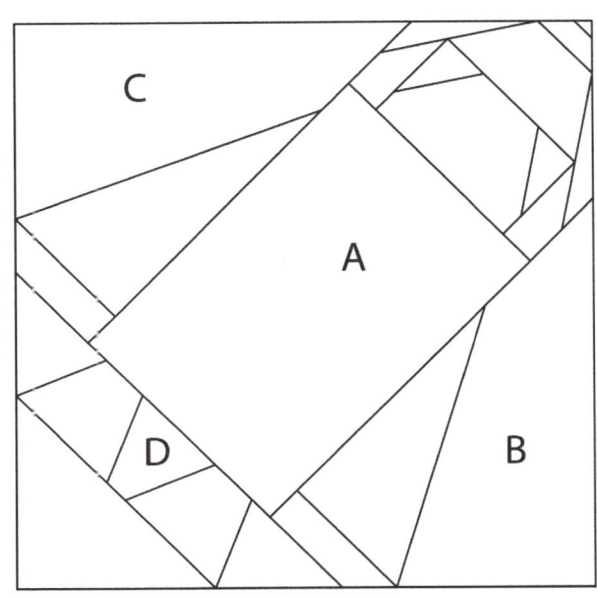

Fabrics:
Blue
Black
Light Gray
Gray
White

Template: Page 39
Difficulty: Level 2

Section A:
1-Black	5-Blue	9-Black
2-Blue	6-Blue	10-White
3-Blue	7-White	11-Blue
4-Blue	8-White	

Section B:
1-Lt Gray	2-Black	3-White

Section C:
1-Lt Gray	2-Black	3-White

Section D:
1-White	3-Gray	5-White
2-Gray	4-White	6-White

Beach Ball

- - - - - - - - -

Fabrics:
Red
Green
Yellow
White

Template: Page 40
Difficulty: Level 3

Section A:
1-Green   3-Red   5-Yellow
2-White   4-White

Section B:
1-Green   4-White   7-White
2-White   5-White
3-Red   6-Yellow

Section C:
1-Green   4-White   7-White
2-White   5-White
3-Red   6-Yellow

Section D:
1-Green   3-White   5-White
2-Red   4-Yellow

Section E:
1-Green   3-White   5-White
2-Red   4-Yellow

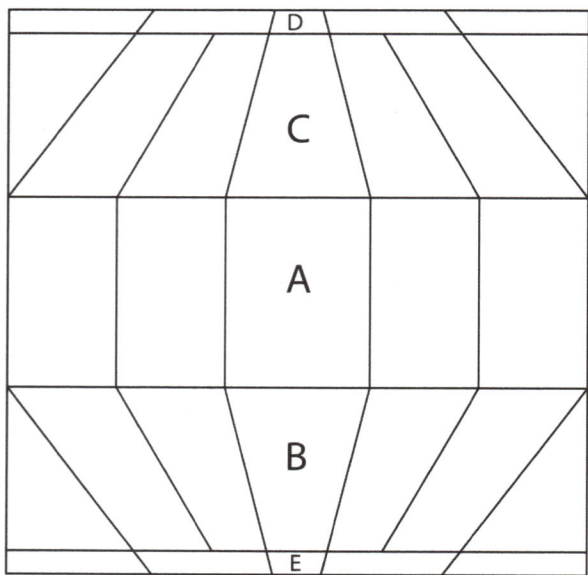

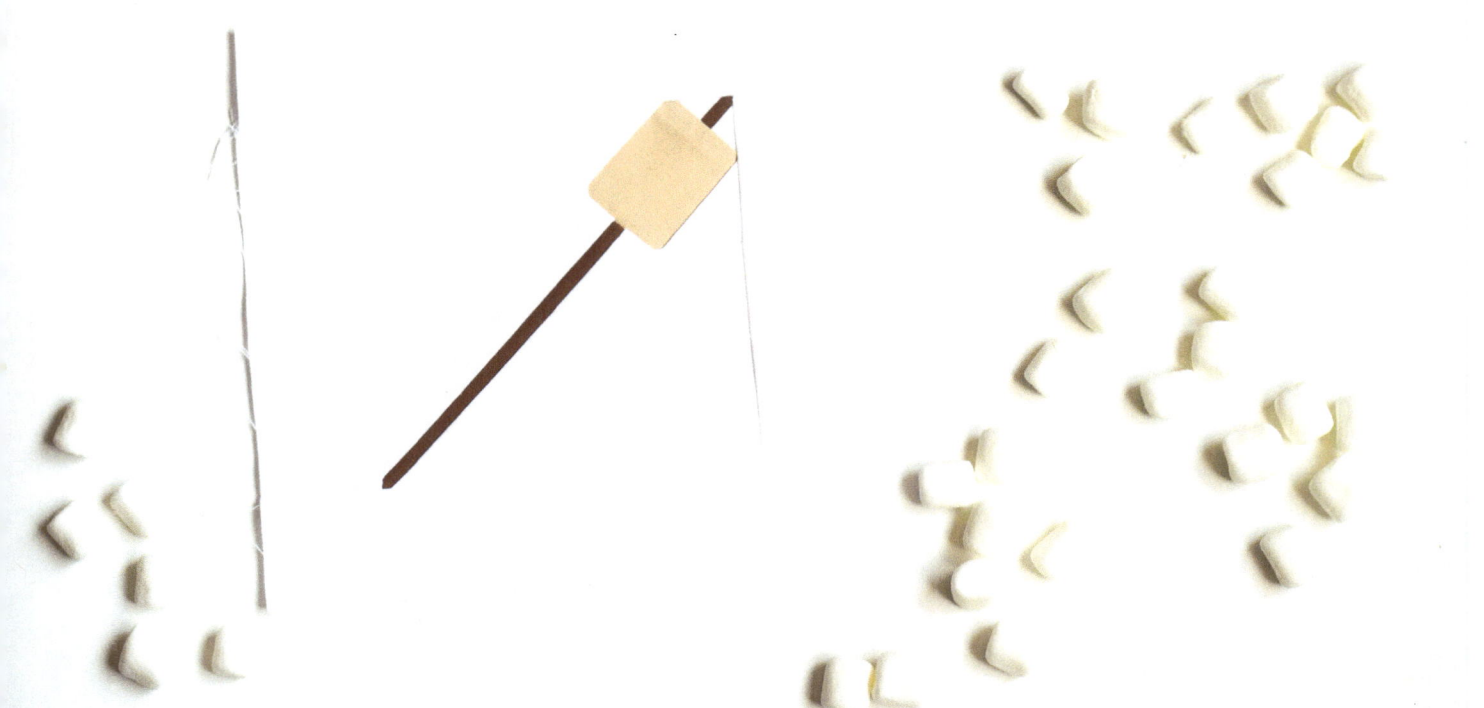

Roasted Marshmallow

Fabrics:
Brown
Tan
White

Template: Page 40
Difficulty: Level 1

Section A:
1-Brown	4-Tan	7-White
2-White	5-White	8-White
3-White	6-White	

Section B:
1-Brown	2-White	3-White

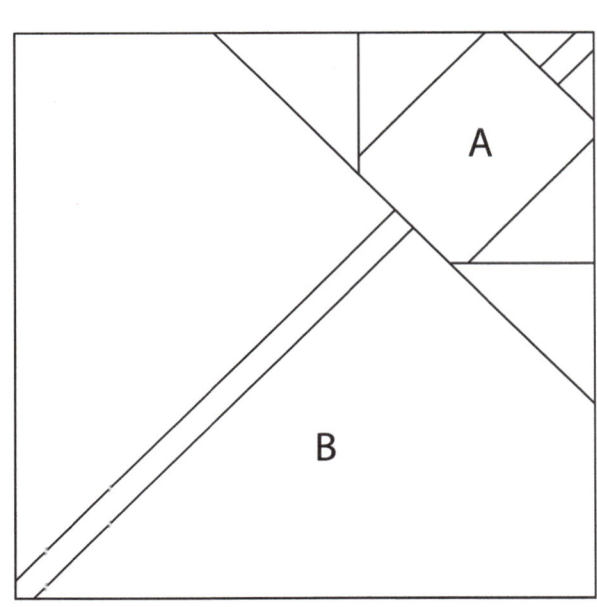

Sand Pail

Fabrics:
Orange
White

Template: Page 41
Difficulty: Level 2

Section A:
1-White	5-Orange	9-White
2-Orange	6-Orange	10-White
3-Orange	7-White	11-Orange
4-Orange	8-White	

Section B:
1-Orange   2-White   3-White

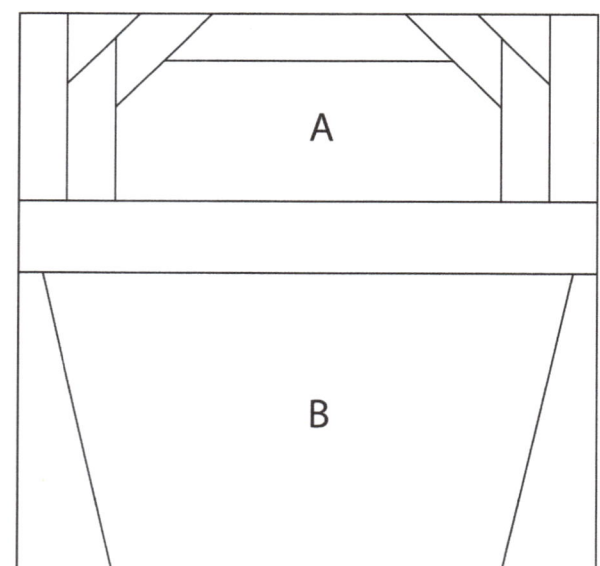

Flashlight

Fabrics:
Blue
Light Gray
Yellow
White

Template: Page 41
Difficulty: Level 2

Section A:
1-Lt Gray
2-Blue
3-Blue
4-Blue
5-Blue
6-White
7-White
8-White

Section B:
1-Blue
2-White
3-White
4-White
5-White

Section C:
1-Yellow
2-White
3-White

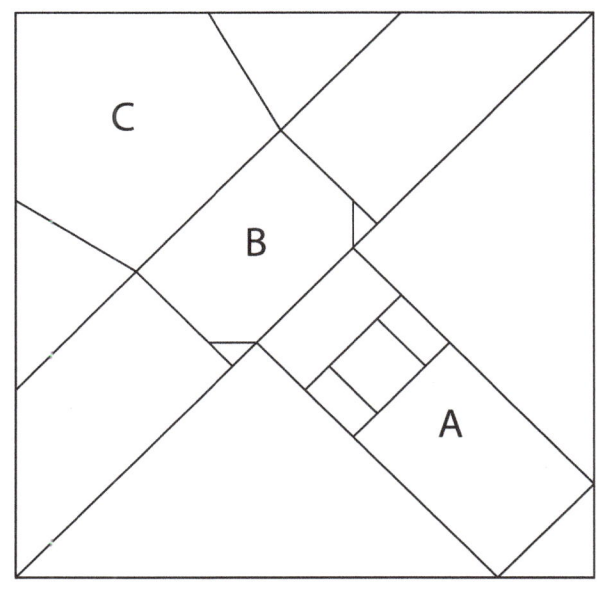

Umbrella

Fabrics:
Purple
Blue
Green
Yellow
Red
Gray
White

Template: Page 42
Difficulty: Level 2

Section A:
1-Green	4-White	7-Red
2-Blue	5-White	8-White
3-Purple	6-Yellow	9-White

Section B:
1-Gray	2-White	3-White

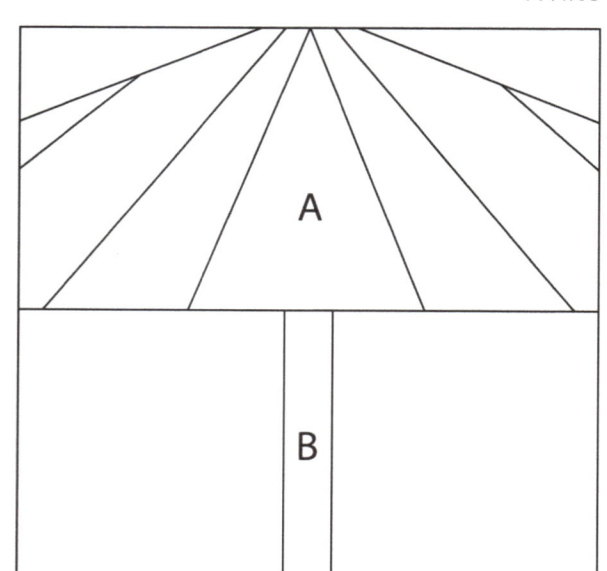

Sand Castle

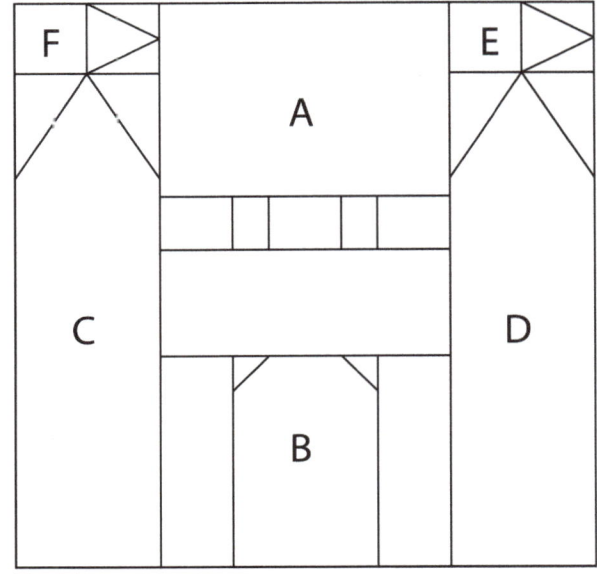

Note: Sew F to C and E to D before sewing to AB

Fabrics:
Tan
Light Tan
Blue
White

Template: Page 42
Difficulty: Level 3

Section A:
1-Lt Tan	3-White	5-Lt Tan
2-White	4-Lt Tan	6-White

Section B:
1-Tan	3-Lt Tan	5-Lt Tan
2-Lt Tan	4-Lt Tan	6-Lt Tan

Section C:
1-Tan	2-White	3-White

Section D:
1-Tan	2-White	3-White

Section E:
1-Blue	3-White	4-White
2-White		

Section F:
1-Blue	3-White	4-White
2-White		

Tent

Fabrics:
Green
Dark Green
Gray
White

Template: Page 43
Difficulty: Level 1

Section A:
1-Gray
2-Dk Green
3-Dk Green
4-Green
5-Green
6-Green
7-Green
8-Green
9-White
10-White

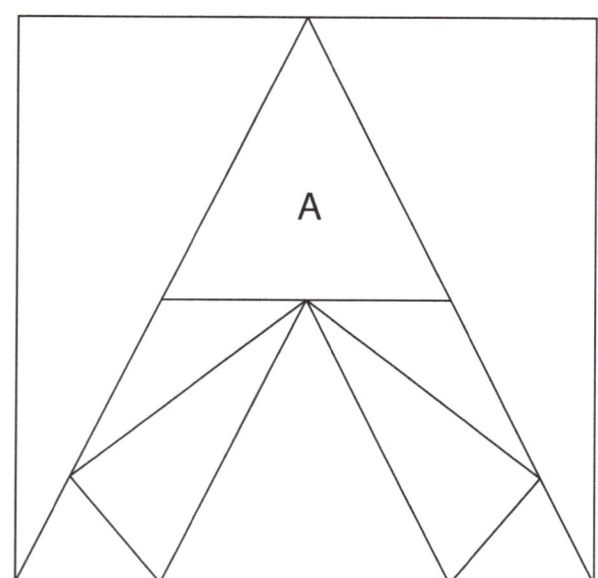

Volcano

Fabrics:
Brown
Red
Gray
White

Template: Page 43
Difficulty: Level 2

Section A:
1-Red
2-Brown
3-Red
4-Brown
5-Brown
6-Red
7-Brown
8-Red
9-Brown
10-White
11-White

Section B:
1-Gray
2-White
3-White
4-White
5-White

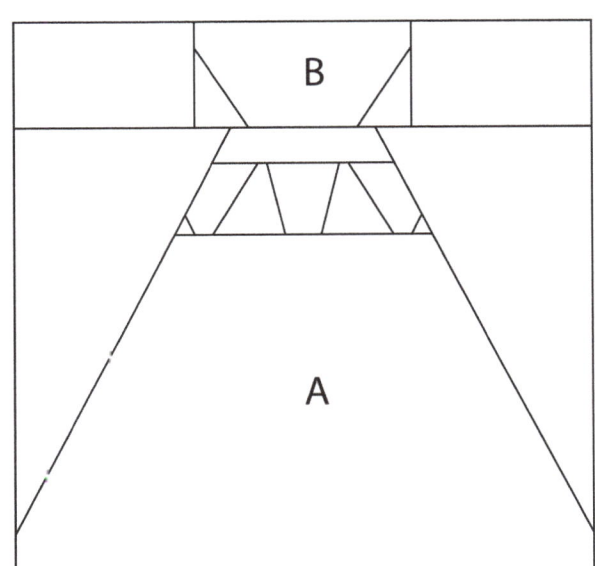

Campfire

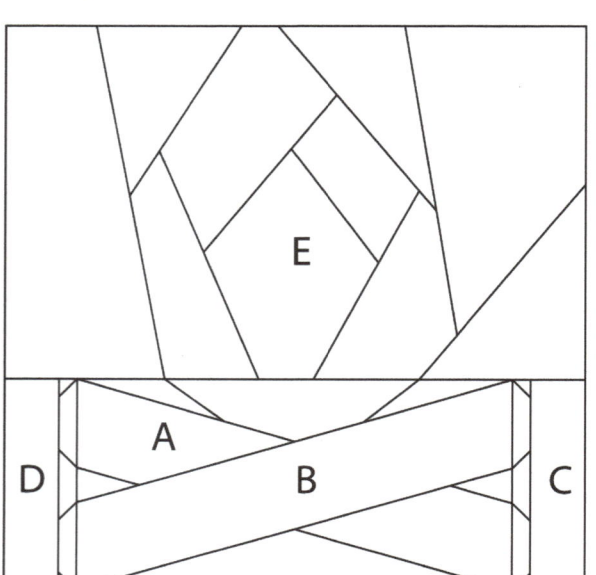

Fabrics:
Brown
Dark Brown
Orange
Yellow
White

Template: Page 44
Difficulty: Level 3

Section A:
1-White
2-Yellow
3-White
4-Brown
5-White

Section B:
1-White
2-Brown
3-White
4-Dk Brown

Section C:
1-White
2-Brown
3-Dk Brown
4-White
5-White
6-White

Section D:
1-White
2-Dk Brown
3-Brown
4-White
5-White
6-White

Section E:
1-Orange
2-Yellow
3-Yellow
4-Yellow
5-Yellow
6-White
7-White
8-White
9-White
10-White

Popsicle

Fabrics:
Red
Light Red
Tan
White

Template: Page 45
Difficulty: Level 3

Note: Sew A to B, and C to D, then combine.

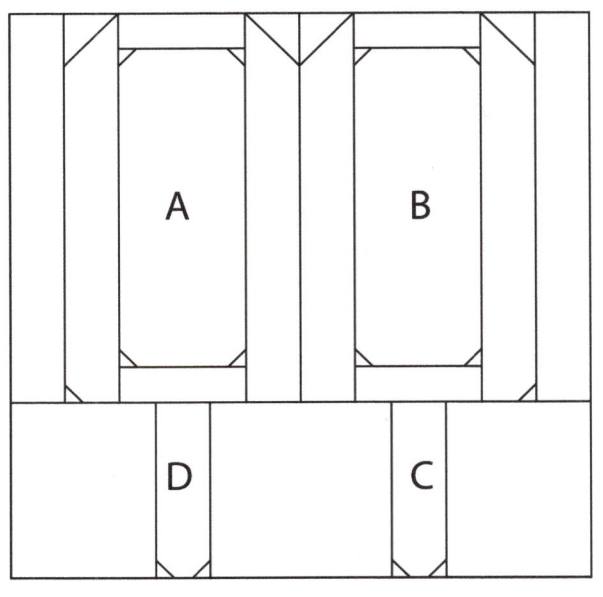

Section A:
1-Lt Red
2-Red
3-Red
4-Red
5-Red
6-Red
7-Red
8-Red
9-Red
10-White
11-White
12-White
13-White

Section B:
1-Lt Red
2-Red
3-Red
4-Red
5-Red
6-Red
7-Red
8-Red
9-Red
10-White
11-White
12-White
13-White

Section C:
1-Tan
2-White
3-White
4-White
5-White

Section D:
1-Tan
2-White
3-White
4-White

Soda Pop

Fabrics:	**Template:** Page 45
Blue	**Difficulty:** Level 1
Cream	
Light Gray	
White	

Section A:
1-Lt Gray	4-White	7-White
2-Blue	5-White	8-White
3-Blue	6-Lt Gray	

Section B:
1-White	3-Cream	5-White
2-Cream	4-White	

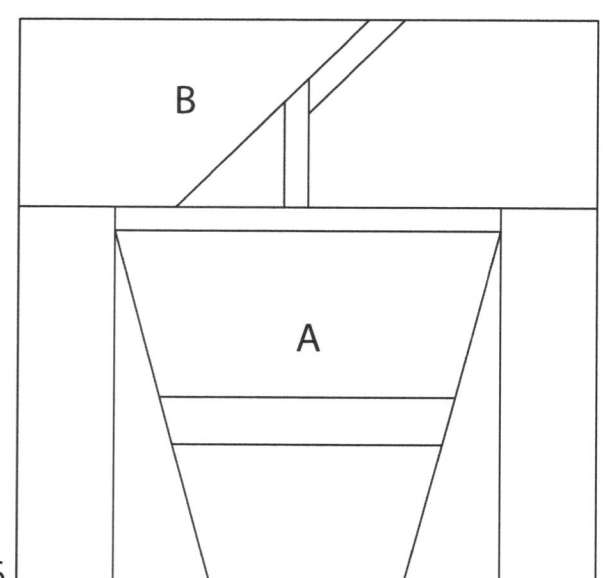

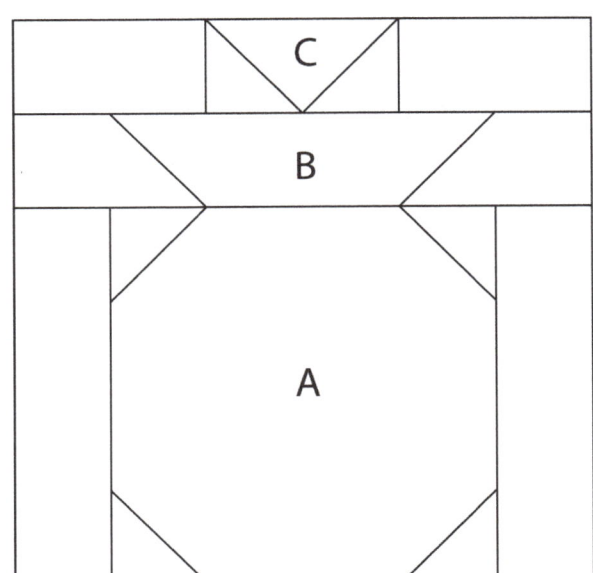

Pineapple

Fabrics:
Yellow
Green
White

Template: Page 46
Difficulty: Level 2

Section A:
1-Yellow	4-White	7-White
2-White	5-White	
3-White	6-White	

Section B:
1-Green   2-White   3-White

Section C:
1-White   3-Green   5-White
2-Green   4-White

Pizza

Fabrics:
Yellow
Red
Tan
White

Template: Page 46
Difficulty: Level 1

Section A:
1-Yellow
2-Red
3-Tan
4-Tan
5-Tan
6-White
7-White
8-White
9-White

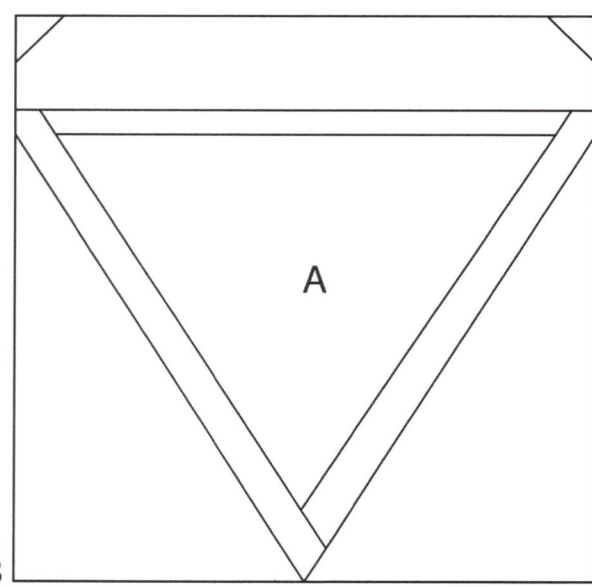

Orange

Fabrics:
Orange
Green
White

Template: Page 47
Difficulty: Level 1

Section A:
1-Orange	4-White	7-White
2-White	5-White	
3-White	6-White	

Section B:
1-Green	3-White	5-White
2-White	4-Green	6-White

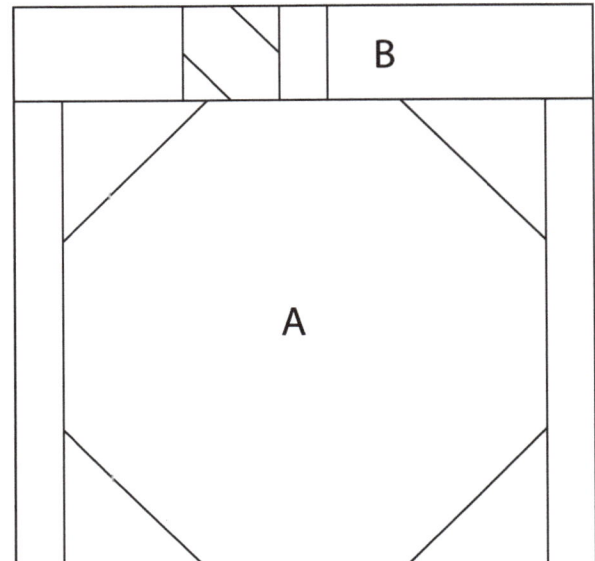

Ice Cream

Fabrics:
Pink
Tan
White

Template: Page 47
Difficulty: Level 2

Section A:
1-Pink	3-White	5-White
2-White	4-White	

Section B:
1-Pink	3-White	5-White
2-White	4-White	

Section C:
1-Tan	2-White	3-White

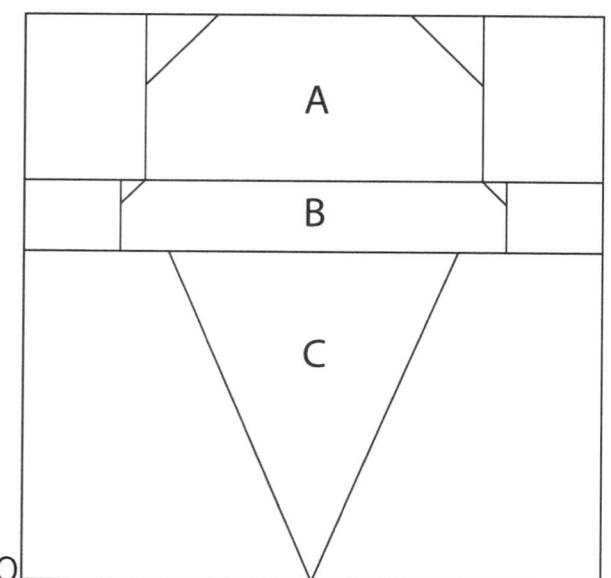

Hot Dog

Fabrics:
Tan
Red
Yellow
White

Template: Page 48
Difficulty: Level 2

Section A:
1-Red
2-White
3-White
4-Yellow
5-Red
6-Yellow
7-Red
8-Yellow
9-Red
10-Yellow
11-Red
12-White
13-White

Section B:
1-Tan
2-White
3-White
4-White
5-White
6-White
7-White
8-White

Section C:
1-Tan
2-White
3-White
4-White
5-White
6-White
7-White
8-White

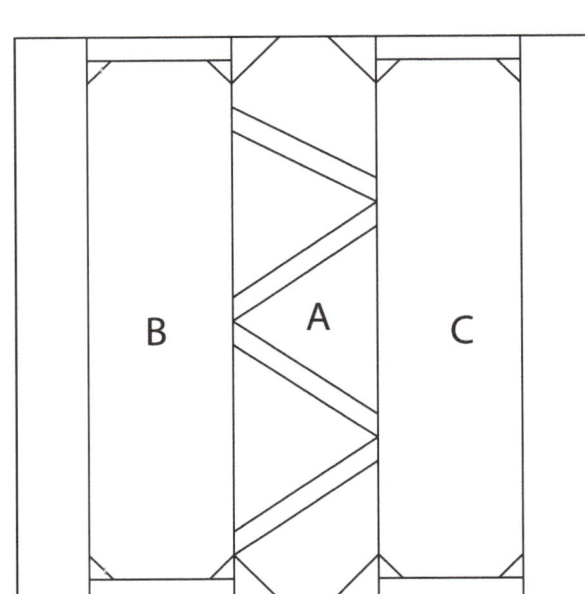

101

Donut

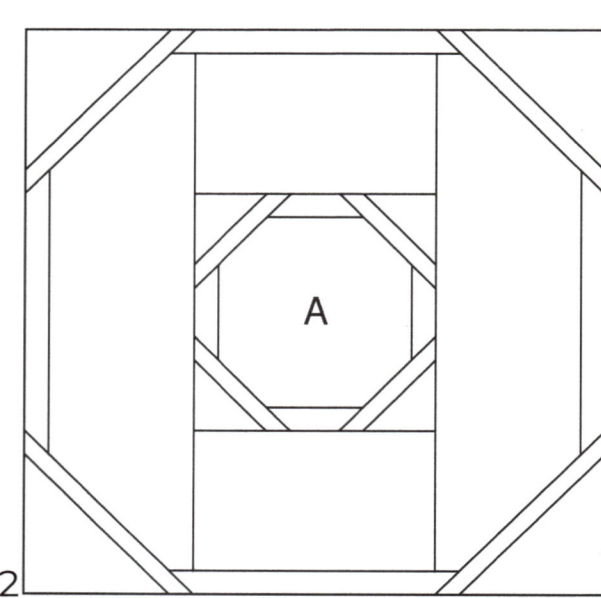

Fabrics:
Pink
Tan
White

Template: Page 48
Difficulty: Level 2

Section A:

1-White	11-Pink	21-Tan
2-Tan	12-Pink	22-Tan
3-Tan	13-Pink	23-Tan
4-Tan	14-Pink	24-Tan
5-Tan	15-Pink	25-Tan
6-Tan	16-Pink	26-White
7-Tan	17-Pink	27-White
8-Tan	18-Tan	28-White
9-Tan	19-Tan	29-White
10-Pink	20-Tan	

Banana

– . – . – . –

Fabrics:
Yellow
Brown
White

Template: Page 49
Difficulty: Level 2

Section A:
1-Yellow   3-White   4-White
2-White

Section B:
1-White   2-Brown   3-White

Section C:
1-Yellow   2-White   3-White

Section D:
1-Yellow   2-White   3-White

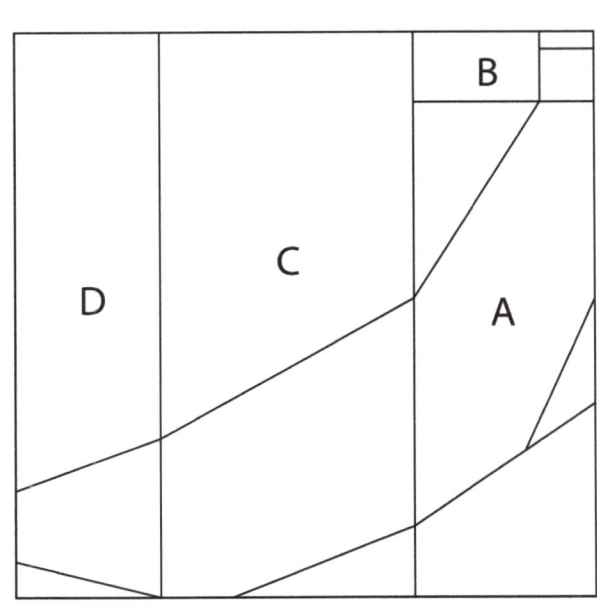

Hamburger

Fabrics:
Tan
Red
Yellow
Brown
Green
White

Template: Page 49
Difficulty: Level 1

Section A:
1-Tan
2-Red
3-Yellow
4-Brown
5-Green
6-Tan
7-White
8-White
9-White
10-White

A

Cotton Candy

o-o-o-o-o

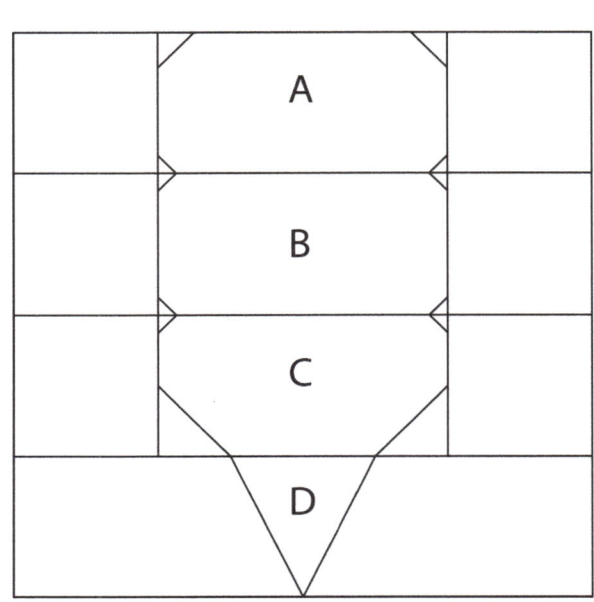

Fabrics:
Light Blue
Light Pink
Tan
White

Template: Page 50
Difficulty: Level 2

Section A:
1-Lt Blue	4-White	7-White
2-White	5-White	
3-White	6-White	

Section B:
1-Lt Pink	4-White	7-White
2-White	5-White	
3-White	6-White	

Section C:
1-Lt Blue	4-White	7-White
2-White	5-White	
3-White	6-White	

Section C:
1-Tan	2-White	3-White

Apple

Fabrics:
Red
Green
White

Template: Page 50
Difficulty: Level 2

Section A:
1-Red   3-White   5-Green
2-White   4-White

Section B:
1-Red   3-White   5-Green
2-White   4-White

Section C:
1-Green   3-White   5-White
2-White   4-Green   6-White

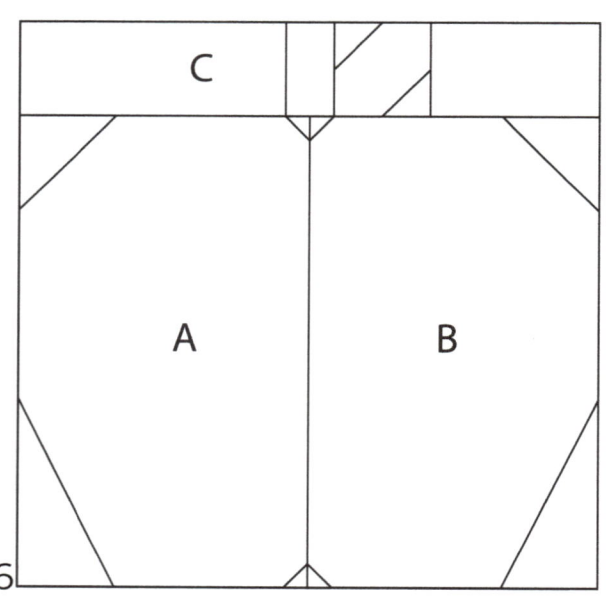

Turkey Leg

Fabrics:
Brown
Tan
White

Template: Page 51
Difficulty: Level 2

Section A:
1-Brown	4-White	7-White
2-White	5-White	8-White
3-White	6-White	

Section B:
1-Brown	2-White	3-White

Section C:
1-Tan	2-White	3-White

Section D:
1-Tan	3-White	5-White
2-White	4-White	6-White

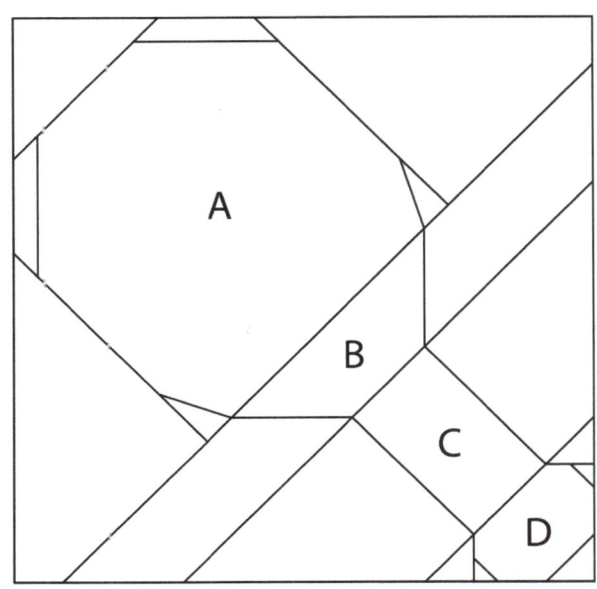

107

Watermelon

Fabrics:
Red
Green
Black
White

Template: Page 51
Difficulty: Level 1

Section A:
1-Black
2-Red
3-Black
4-Red
5-Red
6-Black
7-Red
8-Red
9-Green
10-Red
11-Green
12-Green
13-White
14-White
15-White
16-White

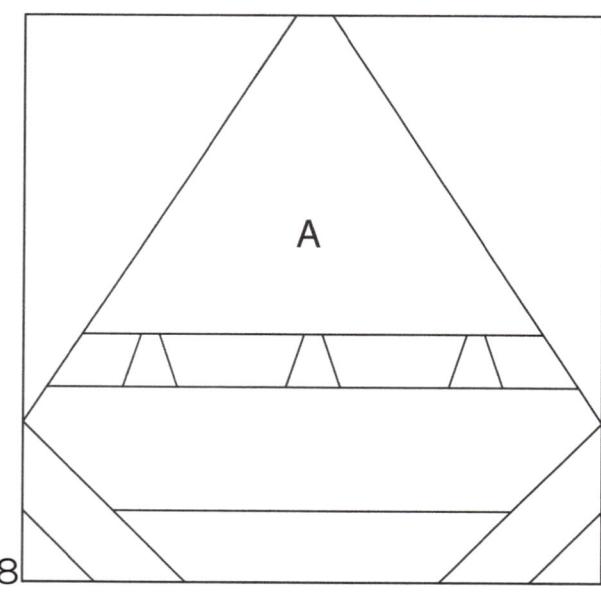

Strawberry

Fabrics:
Red
Green
White

Template: Page 52
Difficulty: Level 2

Section A:
1-Green	6-Red	11-White
2-Red	7-Green	12-White
3-Green	8-Red	13-White
4-Red	9-White	14-White
5-White	10-Red	

Section B:
1-White
2-Green
3-White
4-White

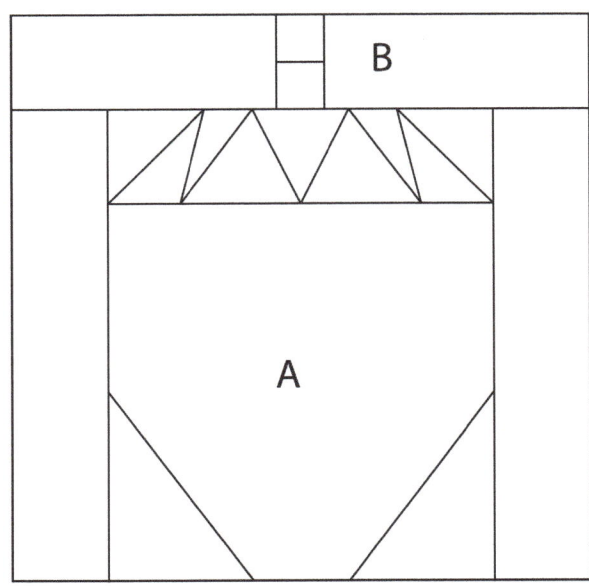

Putting It All Together

Blocks are done and now it's time to sew them all together!

Cutting Instructions

Sashing and Borders

- Cut 28 – 1 ½" White strips
    Sew 17 of the strips together to create
        2 – 1 ½ x 51 ½" White Top/Bottom Border #1 strips
        2 – 1 ½ x 49 ½" White Side Border #1 strips
        9 – 1 ½ x 49 ½" White sashing strips
    Cut remaining into 90 – 1 ½ x 4 ½" White sashing strips

Assembly Instructions

- Arrange your blocks in rows of 10. You will have 10 rows of 10. There is no particular order for this quilt so it is completely up to you how you want to lay them out.

- Sew 1 – 1 ½ x 4 ½" White sashing strip in between each of the blocks in the row
    Your rows should end up being 49 ½" long each

- Sew the rows together with 1 – 1 ½ x 49 ½" White sashing strip between each row

- Sew 1 – 1 ½ x 49 ½" White Border #1 strip to each side of the quilt

- Sew 1 – 1 ½ x 51 ½" White Border #1 strip to the top and bottom of the quilt

- Add back, quilt and bind

Quilting Ideas:

Now that your quilt top is finished, it's time to quilt it! I wouldn't worry about going too crazy and would pick a simple all over pattern. With all the fun pictures in the quilt, this is a quick and easy choice that looks great.

Due to all the tiny blocks and lots of seams, choose something that is a little denser to give the most stability over time. You could also echo around the different shapes and inside the different sections to really highlight all those cute items and animals.

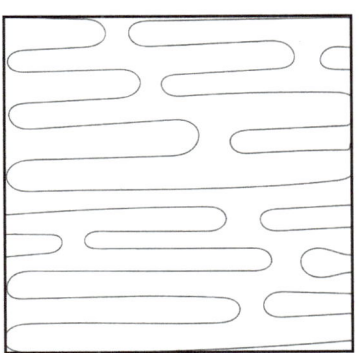
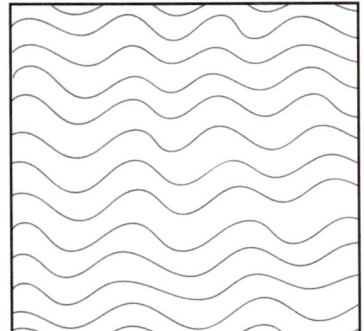

Want a different size?

If you want your finished quilt to be a different size, you have a few options

You can always take away or duplicate blocks.

Another easy solution would be to make the sashing bigger. If you do this, just make sure to grab extra fabric to account for that.

Last, adding extra borders is another quick and easy way to make a quilt bigger. Decide how big you want them and how many for endless possibilites!

111

www.ingramcontent.com/pod-product-compliance
Lightning Source LLC
Chambersburg PA
CBHW041059070526
44579CB00002B/8